Reviews of *Living a Miracle*

"A refreshing and very honest approach from one who is an overcomer. Randy Sims presents his problems and victories in a very interesting and personable way. This book will motivate every leader toward faith and hope."
- *Ben Merold, Senior Minister, Harvester Christian Church*

"Never before has a personal story of struggle and positive attitude and perseverance hit home, more than Randy Sims' story of challenges and outcome. He has shown that if we embrace our challenges and use them to bolster our lives rather than allow them to weight us down, we will live a fuller, more meaningful life. Randy's story touches your soul, your heart and he tells it as if you were sitting on a park bench listening first hand. You feel the emotions he experienced, the pain he endured and the triumph of success. His story embodies the true American spirit that shows we are a great people not because of who we are, but what we do with what we have been given. The character of a man is based on what they do and how they act in the face of challenges. Randy has given everyone that hears his story a roadmap of how to take challenges head on, stare adversity in the face and triumph over our problems. His message of perseverance, positive attitude and faith is much needed in today's society. After hearing Randy's story, you cannot help but be happy. If ever there was a guide on how to struggle and not lose sight of the true blessing of life, then Randy's story is that guide."
- *Senator Scott T. Rupp*

"Randy - I cannot tell you what reading your book copy has done for my soul. You have a devotional masterpiece here. Your truehearted and wholehearted approach to life and

its significant trials [from age 10 right up to the present] has blessed me and will bless many others for years to come since you have taken the time and trouble to capture the experience in print. - I met Randy Sims while serving as a visiting preacher for the Harvester Christian Church of St. Charles, MO in the summer of 2006. He gave me the Reader's Digest version of his life experience of surviving for years with cystic fibrosis and then finally enduring double lung transplantation surgery. He mentioned his book and requested I read it and perhaps write a line or two of recommendation. I can honestly say that I have not had a more enriching experience devotionally this year [it is August 31st today] than the visual and mental digestion of this text. Rarely am I as moved as I was by this book. Perhaps it is because Randy writes as one who has personally passed through a fiery trial rather than writing from an "arms length" perspective. Mostly I think it is because this book is laced with Holy Spirit power. Do you know anyone facing a life-threatening disease or life-threatening surgery? Are you going through such a life passage yourself? If you are not, good; but, if you live long enough, you will. The point is, we all need or will need the impact the chapters of this book can have on us, especially chapter 11 [Why Me?] and chapter 13 [Never Ever Give Up]."
- *Ken Idleman Chancellor, Ozark Christian College*

"Randy Sims writes in simple prose, but his message is as dramatic as it is uncomplicated. Don't give up. Stay positive. This is more than a first-person book. He gives plenty of examples. What might seem to be bad luck might be part of a higher plan, and he talks about a job-seeker who thought he was going to get a job, but didn't. The company? Enron. But still, the most inspirational stories are his own. Diagnosed with cystic fibrosis at the age of 10, he managed

to live a normal life. He went to high school and played golf. He graduated from college. Then his lungs began to fail. He was put on the transplant list, and he got a call at 4:45 in the morning. It's a dramatic story."
- *Bill McClellan Columnist, St. Louis Post-Dispatch*

"Randy Sims is an amazing example of perseverance against all odds. Relying on his faith in God and the love of his family, Randy's story is an encouragement to anyone facing struggles in their life. Randy's story is genuine and expresses much gratitude to those who have helped him along the way, with a special tribute to the family who gave him the precious gift of a second chance at life, his donor family. Randy has chosen to respond to his struggles in a way that is a blessing and encouragement to others and brings honor to his Lord and Savior, Jesus Christ."
- *Merry Smith, LPN, BS Donor Mom, Donor Family*
  Aftercare Coordinator Mid-America Transplant Services

"Randy's book, Living a Miracle, takes us through the demands and rewards of organ transplantation. His work provides a lovely description integrating his life principles and experience while bringing out the human spirit. As a social worker in transplant, 'Living a Miracle' is recommended to anyone wanting to learn more about or considering organ transplantation. Just as the author states 'keeping our chin up is not always the easiest things to do, but when we keep it down, we just keep running into the wall'."
- *Rebecca Bathon, Social Worker, MSW LCSW Lung*
  Transplant and Adult Cystic Fibrosis Program Barnes-
  Jewish Hospital and Washington University School of
  Medicine

LIVING
A
MIRACLE

Turning Your Obstacles into Opportunities

RANDY SIMS
Double-Lung Transplant Recipient

Printed in the United States of America

Published by WingSpan Press, Livermore, CA
www.wingspanpress.com

The WingSpan name, logo and colophon are the trademarks of WingSpan Publishing.

EAN 978-1-59594-084-4
ISBN 1-59594-084-7

First Edition 2006

Library of Congress Control Number: 2006933445

Ask little out of life
And that is what you will receive
Feeling you are just mediocre
And that is what you will believe.

So start pushing yourself a little
And see what you may find
Results will begin appearing in your life
Success starts within in your mind.

Don't take for granted your talents
The potential you have inside
Keep pushing through the obstacles
And let faith become your guide.

For when you've beaten your challenge
And your cynics you have ignored
All that hard work has paid off
You're ready to reap your reward.

Randy Sims

About the author

Randy Sims was diagnosed at the age of 10 with a life threatening disease that left him and his family uncertain of his future, and his life in general.

Randy says, "it really comes down to two choices in life when you are dealt a difficult situation, to give up, or not to give up"; he chose not to give up.

At the age of 31 his disease took him on a unique journey, he would be listed and put on a national waiting list to receive a double-lung transplant.

Randy now focuses on writing and speaking to audiences on why you should not give up, and what we need to do when we face these crises that life may throw our way. It is his desire to encourage you to reach your goals in all your life situations.

His message is inspiring and from the heart. His personal goal is to help others, just as so many have helped him in his life.

In the summer of 2000, Randy's transplant story was featured on CNN Headline News.

http://www.livingamiracle.com/

Acknowledgements

There are really too many people for me to possibly thank in my life.

But a start would be:

I want to express my indescribable gratitude to the anonymous donor family who made a very gracious and unselfish decision in 1999, which led to my second chance at life.

To my wonderful wife and family, as well as my extended church family, for providing a tremendous amount of support and encouragement.

To the entire staff at Barnes-Jewish Hospital in St. Louis, MO for their outstanding care and compassion.

And, of course, I thank God for all the opportunities in life that He has revealed to me, and for providing daily strength to get through it all.

Contents

Chapter 1 It's Your Miracle To Pursue And To Live. 1

Chapter 2 Making The Best Out Of "Change" 11

Chapter 3 Addressing The Attitude. 25

Chapter 4 Rally Time 35

Chapter 5 "A Plan For You" 43

Chapter 6 In Life's Waiting Room 49

Chapter 7 The Call 59

Chapter 8 Using Your Abilities. 77

Chapter 9 Overcoming The Obstacles 85

Chapter 10 Setting and Achieving Your Goals 91

Chapter 11 Why Me? 97

Chapter 12 Dealing With Those In Need 107

Chapter 13 Never Ever Give Up. 113

Chapter 14 Celebrating. 119

Chapter 15 A Special Tribute 127

CHAPTER 1

It's Your Miracle To Pursue And To Live

Galatians 6:9

[9] Let us not become weary in doing good, for at the proper time we will reap a harvest if we do not give up.

Imagine being diagnosed at the age of ten with a disease that led doctors to inform your family that there may only be a couple of years left to live. What a powerful message of how precious life is. You also develop a unique grasp on your priorities in life.

We have all been given a miracle. It is the miracle of creation. Some life spans are longer than others, but some are lived in a much more fulfilling and productive way than others. Unfortunately, it seems common that we take life for granted. Why? Well, probably because we figure everyone else has the same thing that we have. Everyone was born. Everyone we see each day was brought into this world the same way. But, our being created was no accident. We are all here for a reason. Each of us has an abundance of good to offer. We all have specific opportunities that lie in our future. So, what you do with it is up to you.

What determines what you do with your life will be made up of many factors. Some may be as simple as who you choose to associate with. Do you want to be with people who are going to be a positive influence and encourage you to go after and chase your goals? Do you want to be with the kind of people who will challenge you to be your best and reach your potential? People who are willing to give us some good constructive criticism to help us improve ourselves and get us to where we want to be in life, or is it easier to hang out with the crowd that will accept mediocrity? Another factor that determines the outcome of your life is what you are filling your mind with each day. What you read, watch on TV, the kind of conversations we are engaged in will mold us one way or another. What kind of goals you are setting for yourself, or are you even setting goals? That is another important factor. How about your attitude? What we project to others around us and the legacy we strive to leave each day is going to have a major impact on how we live out our 'miracle'. Your faith is also a huge factor. Many of the choices you make will be determined by faith alone.

Maybe even how you were brought up or treated by others when you were young will also have an impact on your future in life. But I don't believe that can ever be a long lasting effect. Who we are comes from within and not from the outside. Sure, what others do or say to us can have a temporary impact on our lives and change how we feel about ourselves, but that which is inside of us is going to be greater and stronger than these outside factors.

So, how do you make the most of this God-given miracle that each of us has been given? How do you choose the right paths in life? How can you be the most fulfilled, successful, and how can you prosper? There is no doubt, none, that you can take control, and that you can make a difference. We are not simple reactive beings, acting as puppets; we have the power and ability to be proactive in our future. We can rise to the level we want to achieve.

Does this mean that every one of us could instantly become a world-renowned surgeon if we all wanted to? That's a good question. First, not all of us desire to become a surgeon. Second, and a big mistake that is often made, "could we instantly become something we wanted to become?" Many people feel that just because they have a goal that it is instantly attainable, hoping that it will just come to them easily without any hardships and hard work along the way. Rarely does something so sought after just fall into our laps. And, how fulfilling would life be if everything we wanted was immediately handed over to us? There is a lot of gratification that comes to us through our efforts, sometimes, more gratification from the efforts than the results. Another consideration is looking at what we are best equipped to become in life. Yes, I believe that it is probably possible to become whatever we want to become in life, but I also feel that we may be better off to evaluate our situation, our goals, and determine a path that makes sense for us. For example, we are all born to become a certain height, and if we desire to be a professional athlete that is usually within a certain size range, it may not be our best intention to spend all our time to go after that one specific sport if we already have a major obstacle against us. Can it be done? Of course. You would just need to be prepared to work harder and spend more time than others whom you would be competing against. But if we are 6 feet tall, becoming a jockey in professional horse racing might not be the best goal, or if we are 5 feet tall, going for the NBA will obviously present more challenges. So, maybe the 5-foot person would do himself or herself more good to look into horse racing?

Back to the surgeon example, if everyone in the word did become a surgeon we would have a pretty imbalanced world. Look at how God created our animal kingdom and plant kingdom, very balanced, a purpose for each. As a much more intelligent being, we should be able to learn from that. Now, don't get me wrong we all need to have desires and determination to get us to those goals, but we also need to think through the goals and make the best decision before we go after them. We also need to feel honored and proud of whom we are and the potential we have. We need to strive to make a positive impact on life regardless of what specific God-given talents we have.

I'm sure there are surgeons who have walked out onto a farm at some point and admired the beauty surrounding them and wished they had chosen a profession that would have allowed them to be out in the fresh air, a farmer, working the soil and producing agriculture that would nourish and take care of the world. I'm sure there have also been farmers who have walked into a hospital and thought how nice it would have been being able to work in a sanitary, temperature-controlled environment and in a profession that was dedicated to taking care of sick people.

Once we have accepted who we are and the positive impact we can make, we will begin to achieve much more out of life. It really does not matter what we do but how we do it and the impact we are making on others in going about our choices. When you start spending your time looking at others around you and feeling their accomplishments are greater than yours instead of focusing on the great impact you can make, that is when your life will become unbalanced. "The one thing we can be that no one else can be, is to be ourselves". So, let's take who we are and what we do and give it our all. Just like the surgeons and farmers, we all need them both desperately. Hopefully we can all appreciate our own value and contributions. Looking at people around us and wondering, "what if I was more like them" or "if I could have only made their choices…." First of all, we never know what someone else is going through or dealing with, many times we only see the glamorous side, which is what we see from the outside. I am sure if a farmer and a surgeon had a discussion about what frustrated them regarding their careers, they would see things they had not thought of before. These thoughts of wishing we were someone else only becomes a distraction to our own lives and keeps us from reaching our own potential.

Have you ever had a tough week and it seemed like your friends and everyone else around you was just having the best week of their life? Just as something else would fall into place for them something would seem to fall apart for you. Maybe it's several small things that are not working out, or maybe it is something big. You lose your job, they get promoted. Your family experiences a loss of a loved one, they are rejoicing at the birth of their new child. Your marriage is on the rocks, they just returned from an exotic resort where they were joyfully celebrating their anniversary.

Not easy situations to deal with, for sure. And, if we are honest with ourselves, a little hard to be happy for them even though we know our day, our good day, is just around the corner. Life is full of ups and downs. It's our character in the down times that really shows the most about us. It's easy to be upbeat and fun to be around when everything is going great, but not so easy when we are right in the middle of some tough challenges. I know some people who are very good at being "up" even when times are tough. I have a ton of respect for them and they are a real inspiration, allowing us to see that we can get through a difficult situation no matter what life throws at us. I know we can all be like this, getting ourselves to where we can be positive even when we are surrounded by negative. It just takes some work on our part. What we are made of deep inside and our inner abilities are stronger than what is impacting us from the outside. It takes practice, and probably does not come naturally for many people, but the stress and frustration is just going to distract us and cause us less enjoyment in life. We need to work hard not to let the things that we cannot control, have control over us.

See, we all have these "external factors" that can attack us. If you were to just sit in a comfortable chair all day, every day, have someone bring you food and drink, only read positive books, only watch positive and encouraging TV shows, never needing to face the "real world," you would have it made. We could even go so far as to only let your friends and family visit when they are in a good mood and only when they didn't have any problems to talk about. Money would just appear in the checking account and the checkbook would always balance to the penny with no problems. Oh, and of course you just felt good, healthy, and full of energy all the time. This would be pretty nice, huh? But if we were honest, really deep down honest with ourselves, we would start getting bored pretty quickly. No challenges to take on and overcome in life? Have you ever wondered what it would be like to physically feel the same all the time? It may sound strange, but the times I went through some very tough health situations, it sure taught me not to take it for granted when I started feeling good again. I sure developed a stronger appreciation for life and an appreciation for being able to do the things I like to do when I started feeling better. I know for a fact that I get more out of life and have more appreciation and enjoyment because of some of the obstacles and challenges I have faced. You sit and have a conversation with someone who has overcome cancer or some other type of difficult, life-threatening challenge, and then talk to someone who has never been sick a day in their life, you will see a big difference in the passion to live and make the most of what they have, I can guarantee you that. That does not mean that we all need to be sick to be happy and fulfilled, that just means we can learn from others around us and make sure we do not fall into a rut of complacency.

Going through our "life challenges" gives each of us the chance to: learn, build character, and to be alive with the opportunity to help and encourage others. Everyone has dealt with something or another, we all face different types of challenges in life. We may look at someone who is struggling through a tough time, and we might wonder why he or she is having so much trouble dealing with it. We may compare it to something we have dealt with and think this should be easy for them to get through. But, we have to remember; everything is different to each person. Plus, they may have never had to deal with something like this before, or had any life experiences to prepare them to cope with what they are going through. You learn from the different experiences that you go through. It is important to remember that it's what you do with what you've learned that is important. Are you going to sit back and let life pass you by or are you going to take action and apply what you have learned to help yourself and others?

Life is a gift. Why would you want to make anything out of it that is less than your best? You have the opportunity to make whatever you want with it, to have life be as successful and fulfilling as possible. When you are looking to move ahead and make the most out of life for yourself, the only person who can tell you that "you can't" is yourself. So start telling yourself that "you can", and then you will.

CHAPTER 2

Making The Best Out Of "Change"

2 Corinthians 4:8–9

[8] We are hard pressed on every side, but not crushed; perplexed, but not in despair; [9] persecuted, but not abandoned; struck down, but not destroyed.

My story starts when I was around the age of ten. I grew up out in the country on a farm. It was a great way to grow up as a kid. Lot's of fun, lots of pets, lots of room to play and explore the great outdoors, beautiful surroundings. I always felt that learning to ride a bike and take a few falls on a gravel road just made us a little tougher. It was my Dad and Mom (Jerry and Margaret) my younger brother, Rick, and myself.

It was at that age that we got some shocking news. It would be news that would change the lives of our whole family. I think many people hear the word "change" or realize they are going to be facing some type of change in their life and automatically feel it is negative. We seem to naturally tend to believe and assume that change can never be good. We hear someone at work say "there's a big meeting at the end of the day, and there is going to be an announcement of some changes coming up…" Probably everyone's heart starts beating a little faster. Everyone jumps on the phone and email trying to find out what's going on. How will this change affect me? Is it a change in the company's benefits, are we facing a merger or downsizing? For those of us who have been caught up in these kinds of drastic changes, it's not always easy to walk out of those meetings with a smile on our face and able to keep our head held high. But, if we think about it, life is full of constant change. It is just that some of it is gradual and some is much more sudden and unexpected. Some is at our choosing and some is out of our control. It's how we deal with it that is going to make a difference and impact our outlook in general. Do we let this change get the best of us? Or, are we willing to take change and make the best out of it? A new challenge and a new beginning!

I've been through those types of sudden changes, but the change that I went through at the age of ten was quite different. At ten years old my parents and doctors were having a difficult time figuring out why I was getting sick so often and having trouble gaining weight. I was in and out of the doctor's offices constantly. After many tests, I was diagnosed with a genetic disorder called cystic fibrosis (CF).

The tests for CF were somewhat of a unique process. They were called 'sweat tests'. I was tested a couple of times in my small town doctor's office, and they came back negative, no CF. To do the test, they just need to collect a sample of sweat, and to do this they put my hand in a plastic bag until it started to perspire. I was later taken to Children's Hospital in St. Louis, this time they taped a small plastic lid to my forearm and then wrapped a diaper around my arm. I was then to walk up and down the hallway several minutes in order to get my arm perspiring. You can get some interesting looks from people when you walk around with a diaper on your arm. This test came back that I did have the disease. It was an emotional shock for all of us.

At that time there were not a lot of good medications or treatments for CF and the doctors told my parents that there was a good chance that I may only have a couple more years to live. Thankfully, my dad and mom didn't just plan for the short term once they were given this news; they planned for a long-term future for me, which included moving off the farm. My dad immediately began working to build us a new home, closer to the city, and away from some of the things on the farm that could be a potential harm for someone with a lung disease. At the time we discovered that I had this hereditary condition we didn't really know anything about it, because none of our family members had CF. It was a situation where carriers of the CF gene had passed it down through the generations. It is pretty rare; only about 30,000 people in the US have it. CF occurs in approximately one of every 3,500 live births of all Americans. It is a disease that attacks the lungs primarily. It also causes problems with the digestion of food, which is why I was not gaining weight as I should. But the issue with the respiratory system is the most serious. CF lungs have a much higher risk of infections due to the way the body's secretions are produced in the lungs. It causes on-going chest congestion which brings on these bouts of chest colds, respiratory infections, and other related problems that continually cause a scarring effect on the lungs. This in turn causes a decline in overall lung function. But, we all lived each day to the fullest, even with this news hanging over our heads. It also seemed to help us not to take things for granted and to have more of an appreciation of life. I tried to take the very best care of myself, and it did cause an adjustment in the entire family's lifestyle to some degree, but we were, and are, a close family and always go through everything together. We were in a true situation of "do your best, and let God take care of the rest". Through prayer, we really turned the entire situation over to God, and on our part, we also did not cut any corners as far as my health and taking care of myself.

I felt very fortunate and blessed, as my symptoms seemed to be appearing that I had a milder form of the disease, but there were still no guarantees of the outcome. There were a lot of things that we had to do behind the scenes to keep it from getting out of control. Lots of "treatments" which involved having someone pound on my back, chest, and sides for about 45 minutes at a time. And this would need to take place anywhere from 1–4 times a day depending how bad my chest was congested. The whole idea behind this was to help keep the airways as open as possible by clearing out the congestion. Otherwise it became very difficult to breathe.

I've heard other CF patients describe breathing as the same feeling as trying to breath though a very skinny straw, like the coffee stirring straws that are very narrow. Along with these treatments was the need for doing special aerosol treatments that involved inhaling medication for about 15–30 minutes before and after the postural drainage treatments. So, I had to always figure on about an extra hour, at least, in the morning before I could head off to school. Oh, there were a lot of pills to be taken too, about 40 to 50 each day. Most of that was medication to help me digest my food. So as you can see I became an expert at pill-taking. Starting in 1976 with this regiment, taking an average of 45 pills a day, and still taking the same amount, ….so 45x365 days in a year, multiply that by the number of years since 1976, I've already reached around the half million mark of pills swallowed.

But other than taking my medicine at school during lunch, no one much knew what was going on with me or what I was dealing with in my life. I didn't talk about it much. They probably wondered why I was coughing all the time though. I tried to cover that up as much as I could. For example, if I was feeling extra congested, I'd just slip off to the restroom and pound on my chest for a few seconds and try to clear my lungs out some.

There always seemed to be some fun things that happened because of having CF though. We lived about 2 ½ hours from St. Louis when I was growing up. St. Louis is also where I was diagnosed and where the CF clinic was that I attended. It was always like a mini vacation to get to go to clinic. It was a treat for the whole family. My parents had a way of making the appointments seem fun because they'd plan some special things along with the trips. We would go out to eat at special places, go up in the St. Louis Arch, shopping, the zoo, that type of thing.

Once my dad got us St. Louis Cardinal baseball tickets for

a game after my clinic visit. While I was in the doctor's office, we mentioned to the doctor that we were heading to the game after we were done. He asked my dad if he could see our tickets and he stepped away for a second and we could see him making a phone call. We had no idea what he was doing or what was going on. About half way through the ball game that night, 2 people from Jack Buck's office (Jack Buck was the great Cardinal announcer and a wonderful person) came to my seat and loaded me up with souvenirs. I still remember they said Mr. Buck would have been over himself, but he was announcing the game. I remember another time we were in St. Louis for my CF clinic. It was 1982 during the World Series. The Cardinals were playing in the Series that year. We didn't have tickets that time, but we spent time walking around the stadium, and I bought a t-shirt that I must have worn constantly for the next ten years or so.

I was fortunate enough that the treatments and medication were working well. I was able to do most things that a guy growing up wanted to do. I enjoyed school, sports, and hanging out with my friends.

My high school days were fun. I was on the school's golf team and earned a varsity letter my sophomore, junior, and senior year. I had a great group of friends, we loved going to all the ball games, school dances, and hanging out on the weekends. College was great too. I might have pushed myself a little too much or too hard at times, but I am the kind of person that likes to stay busy. I double-majored in business, marketing & management. I also worked on an English minor for a while too, but decided I wanted to graduate at some point. I was pretty heavily involved in the activities within the School of Business as well: President of the American Marketing Association, I was appointed to the College Curriculum Committee, on the Dean's Advisory Board, and was also a Graduate Marshall one year. And, besides that, I also worked about 20–30 hours in a retail department store, selling men's clothing. I did end up in the hospital a couple of times while I was in college. Usually for about 15 days at a time. I was having some more severe respiratory problems, so they used IV medications to help clear my lungs, along with much more aggressive treatments and therapies.

I got used to eating hospital food, even enjoyed some of it. I always looked forward to the part of the day, while in the hospital, when they would bring my menu in for me to fill out what I wanted for each meal for the following day. Pretty neat to go through and pick out from all these choices: your drink, entrée, desserts, and salads. And I think I got to be a pro at what to watch out for and what I knew was going to be good. I also learned pretty quickly that sometimes you could actually write in an optional choice that was not on the menu, and they'd bring it up to you.

Also, once I started feeling better and the IV antibiotics were beginning to work I was allowed to go out on a "pass". Which was nice for me, not living in St. Louis at the time it gave me a chance to do a little sight seeing while being admitted in the hospital. I would go to the zoo, St. Louis Science Center, Union Station, and some of the other interesting landmarks in the area. Sometimes, someone from the hospital staff would go along with me, or my family would take me out when they came to visit. I'll never forget one time a medical student took me out for the afternoon to the St. Louis Zoo. When I got back to the hospital my family had arrived to visit, and since I was gone over the lunch service, I found my little brother in my hospital bed helping himself to my lunch. That is a fun memory. The times I was in the hospital in college ended up not really being a big hindrance to my schedule. I was able to get caught up pretty easily in my course requirements.

I enjoyed college, and always felt much better once I had

these "tune-ups" in the hospital. College was even more fun when I felt good.

Post college, I actually found myself relocating to St. Louis. I had taken a job there in retail management. For the next ten years or so, things were kind of up and down as far as my health. I would go a few years without having any health issues or flair-ups with CF. Almost forgetting I had to deal with it, other than the daily routines, but then it would rear its head again. Once I started a career after college it was more difficult for me when I had to be hospitalized. It was difficult because I always hated missing work. But, I knew it needed to be done so I made the best of it knowing there was no other option. Also, I knew I would feel much better and stronger, and be more productive when I came out of the hospital. It was really something else, I almost felt like a new person once I was done with a ten to fifteen day hospital stay. I always looked forward to that feeling. And, with the advances of healthcare, and specifically home healthcare, I was able to take the IV antibiotics through a home-health company instead of needing to be admitted into the hospital each time.

A nurse would come to my house and start the IV and leave all the supplies that I needed to administer the medication myself. This was great. I could actually put on a suit, and have an IV catheter in my arm, and run the line up into my sleeve and then inside the chest pocket of my suit coat. The medicine was in a tightly wound plastic ball mechanism and it would automatically push the antibiotics through the tubing and into a vein in my arm. So, believe it or not, I could be in a meeting, or even shaking hands with someone, and they would have no idea that just a few inches from their hand all this was going on. It made my life much easier than being in the hospital all the time. It usually ran pretty smooth. When it was time to hook myself up to a new dose, I'd go out to my car in order to have some privacy and hook up another vial of the medication, then head back into work. Then in an hour or so it was done, and I'd run back out to the car and disconnect it. Since the medications were pretty strong, the IV lines only lasted around 3–4 days, sometimes only a day or so. Then I'd have to have a nurse come back to my house and start a new line. But, it was just one of those things that I adjusted into my schedule. Sometimes it was a real easy process to have a new line started, sometimes, it was not so easy. Plus, with having so many in my arms over the years (I estimate around 250) my veins became a little more challenging for the nurses to get a "good stick". I'll never forget one day at work. I left my office to visit a client where we had contract employees working. I was delivering their payroll to them. My IV went out; basically it started burning at the site, which meant it was no longer in the vein the right way. It happened right during the time a dose of medication was being administered. Basically, what happens is it erodes the vein out in that specific area. Well, I needed to get something done. I did not want to miss a dose of medicine and I also needed to get the burning IV fixed too. And, I also had about 100 employees ready to get their Friday paycheck. Lucky for me, there was a home health office on the way to my client's location, and they would have all the necessary equipment there to start a new line for me. I called on my way there and they had someone waiting for me when I arrived to take care of me. I knew I only had about 30 minutes or so to keep myself from being late to deliver payroll. The first option was to try and put a PICC line in. It is a longer catheter, about 6–10 inches, and it lasts longer than a normal IV line. I was in the treatment room and there were two nurses working to try and get this going for me. They got the old line out, and started working to get a new one started. The problem was, I apparently had not been drinking enough water and was a little dehydrated.

That always makes it tougher to get the line into the veins. I remember the one nurse trying 2 or 3 times in one arm, with no luck. Of course, I was watching the clock out of the corner of my eye. But at the same time, I sure did not want to make them feel nervous or that I was putting any pressure on them! They were both very nice. Then the other nurse said she'd work on the other arm at the same time. Kind of like they were in a race to see who could get everything working first. Which was fine with me. My mind was just focused on getting back to work. One finally voiced those great words "there we go" which I knew meant the needle was in and the catheter threaded OK and the IV fluid was flowing the way it should. Well, my arms were a little sore and pretty messy, I had not taken time to take my watch off and I remember them helping me to get the blood cleaned out of the watchband too. We got everything taken care of and everything was back in working order and I walked into the conference room a minute ahead of schedule. I had a pretty good feeling of self-respect that day. A couple of the employees were always early because they knew I usually arrived before my scheduled time, and they made the comment to me "we were wondering if you were going to make it?" I think the part I liked the most was being the only one knowing what had just happened and what I had gone through in order to get there. Of course, they just all wanted to make sure I got their paycheck to them on time. And I would have felt the exact same way if I were in their shoes. This was a real good lesson for me. We never know what someone has just gone through. We sometimes need to cut people a little slack, because we could be the straw that breaks their back depending what all they've had to encounter that day, week, or month.

For example, someone walks into work in the morning, and seems to be a little short with you, or not their normal self. Our first tendency is to give them the same treatment back, right? That is probably the way we often feel anyway. But, we have no idea what kind of personal or family crisis or problem they are dealing with. In reality, the absolute worst thing we could do to them is to give them the brush off or cold shoulder, or even worse, give them a piece of our mind. It could really push them over the edge. If instead we could maybe just ask them "are you OK today, is there something you want to talk about?" Or, "is there anything I can do for you?" Yeah, we might have to suck up our pride some, but it sure would be better if we could all discipline ourselves to do better in situations like this. We have no idea what kind of support the person we are talking to has at home. They may feel like they have no one to talk to at all. They may feel completely alone, and then they walk into work or school or wherever we encounter them, in line at the grocery store maybe, and if our reaction to them is negative, then they are really going to feel stranded. We would be very surprised how far a kind word can go to someone in a situation like that. Ever stop to think how it makes us feel even when someone takes an extra second out of his or her day to hold an elevator for us, or hold a door open and wait for us to get there? When we start our day each morning, we have a couple of options. One, what kind of mood we are going to be in, and if due to some "external factors" we just can't seem to control our mood, we better believe we can control our attitude. The second option is, what we are going to do for the attitude of others around us. Are we going to be someone that people want to be around because they feel encouraged? Or, are we looking out for no one but ourselves, and feeling like no one had better get in our way?

Might I suggest this? Make it a point each day to build up that person next to you. Stay focused on not only being positive, but doing something positive too. You can be the best positive thinker in the world and have the best positive attitude ever, but if you don't let it out and verbalize it, it's not going to do much good, is it? So, let others hear what you are thinking, and everyone will be better because of it.

CHAPTER 3

Addressing The Attitude

Philippians 4:8

[8] Finally, brothers, whatever is true, whatever is noble, whatever is right, whatever is pure, whatever is lovely, whatever is admirable—if anything is excellent or praiseworthy—think about such things.

Our attitude and outlook in life play such a critical role in how we get through the tough times. When one thing starts to fall apart, do we look at everything as negative, or can we rise above that and see the other positive things that are going on around us?

One of the things that happened to me, especially as my breathing became more difficult, was having blood vessels break in my lungs. Hemoptysis is the medical term for it. Sometimes it would be from getting extremely short of breath, which was happening more often and with less activity. Sometimes it would just happen when I was sitting still and doing nothing. That was usually caused by an area in one of my lungs getting irritated, probably from some type of infection. Once walking from work to my car, it happened, and it was pretty substantial. I was walking up a hill to the parking lot, to get to my car. I started getting short of breath, and started coughing pretty hard. That caused me to start coughing up blood and it was a lot. My white dress shirt was covered with blood. I know it scared me and it did the security guard who was in the parking lot too. It was such a weird feeling when it would happen, kind of like when you would be swimming and get some water sucked down the wrong way. When that happens, you start coughing like crazy, same with this. The security guard came over to me and tried to help. Let me tell you, when you see someone out in public, having a hard time or something has happened to them physically, do the right thing and see if you can help them out. Being alone and having something happening to you, believe me, you would want to have someone reach out to you and help. It's the 'Good Samaritan' thing to do. It's terrible to feel alone when you are having trouble.

I think sometimes we shy away when we see someone in need because we are not sure we would know what to do, just being there is the right thing to do, the rest will fall into place.

Well, I quickly got a hold of my family, and they came rushing to where I was and we made a quick trip to the emergency room. That bought me a ticket to a couple of weeks on the "IV Routine". It was embarrassing to me when I would get sick out in public. Of course, it was pretty dumb to feel that way; it was obviously out of my control. Once, my family and I were at the St. Louis Science Center. I had walked up some steps and it hit me bad then too. I'm sure the people around me thought I was some type of medical-science presentation or something. They probably really did once the paramedics arrived. But, there were a few times I had to deal with this happening at work, it would happen in a shopping center, the movie theater, at home...I got as used to dealing with it as I could.

You know, each morning when we start our day, we probably can assume there will be some things that are going to come along that we are not going to be pleased with. Some days those things might be big issues, some days not so big. But, we have a conscious decision to make of how we will deal with them. By taking a look in the mirror at your overall attitude, you can probably get a pretty good idea of how you will respond to a crisis, whether it is major or minor. I've seen people fly off the handle just because they dropped a book or something on the ground. And then I've seen other people be in a major issue, maybe a car accident or something like that, and remain as calm and polite as if nothing happened.

We've all heard the saying "attitude adjustment". I love that saying. I often tell my wife when I am having a bad day that I just need to give myself an attitude adjustment. Wouldn't that be great, if we could somehow pop our attitude back in place, just like when we twist or stretch our back or neck and it feels better? Well, we all have two choices when we put our first foot on the floor each morning. First we should be filled with gratitude that we have another day to enjoy. And, if we really think about it, we really do have a choice of what kind of day we are going to make it out to be. Thinking in that way will help you to make a conscious effort to make it the best day possible. There are things that we can do to start the day off right. Prayer is the number one thing that gets me going in the right direction. That way, I know I don't have to deal with my problems alone as they come up during the day. Keep this up consistently, and you will see results.

I think many times, some people get their day started with a big "pity party". Thinking whatever stress or burden you may be dealing with is something that no one else has any idea about or could ever possibly understand. And, no one else could possibly be facing this same kind of issue. Wouldn't it be great to be able to see into everyone's minds? We'd probably hear things like: "No one else is having to deal with a family issue like mine, there's no way people around me could understand the way I am feeling, there is no way anyone else could have put up with children like mine, how could anyone have the same kind of homework load that I have, and have to work a full time job too, I'm sure no one else today had their dog have an accident on the carpet just as I was about to walk out the door to work"

That last one might sound funny, but many times it can be the smallest things that will trigger us into starting our day off in a bad way. Can't find the right clothes, the tie won't tie right, bad hair day, lost a shoe, or can't find the darn car keys. Wow, then we jump in the car and at the first intersection someone cuts us off, not good for them, huh.

We'd better do something between then and when we walk into work or school, or wherever we are going, or you can bet the impression we will make on those around us will not be a good one at all! Whether it is a first impression, or people we see everyday, not only are they going to have a poor regard of us, but it will probably make them likely to have a bad start to their day too. It is a real vicious circle, and it can spread like wildfire. Think about it, you walk into work, and you get the wrath of your boss's day starting off bad, then you spread that around to the people that you work with, and they do the same.... When you go out to lunch, you snap at the person taking your order, they give it right back to you, then on the way back to work you tell your co-worker that you sure can't believe the attitude that the waitress had. It keeps brewing the rest of the day, then by the time you get home to your family, guess what, no one wants to be around you, and you infect them with this sour attitude too. Then everyone goes to bed mad and wakes up feeling the same way the next day. It can be a real epidemic.

That's why I always hated those early morning meetings when the person who led the meeting did not have a positive bone in his or her body. I always wanted to stand up and just say, "Thanks for ruining everyone's day". Think how much more fun it would have been if they had started out with a joke, or giving out some kind of reward, or even doughnuts? Doughnuts are always nice.

So, what do we do when we leave the house and it is one of "those" mornings? Couldn't find anything we needed if our life depended on it. We got dressed and realized at that last critical second as we are rushing out the door that our socks don't match. Man, now that can be a crisis. Well, first we better apologize to our spouse, children, parents, or whoever we live with. Better include the pet too, no need to ruin their day. Then, start filling yourself with some "positive nourishment". If all we ever ate was junk food, and sat around on the couch all day, think what our energy level would be like and how we'd feel. Our mind is no different. We need to feed the good, positive stuff into it too. And exercise it appropriately. Our emotional make up really deserves as much attention as our physical. Maybe even more, because it's our mental attitude that can play a big part in how we feel physically. We are giving ourselves a double benefit when we do that.

So, be careful what you are pumping into your mind everyday. Just like food, the better it is the better we feel. Start looking at it like this each day: who can we talk to, who can we hang out with, what can we watch on TV, what can we read, what can we listen to on the radio... that is going to have a good, strong positive impact on how we feel. How will each of these choices we make determine what kind of attitude we will have? We have to take a proactive approach on handling our own frame of mind. No one is going to do it for us, these are conscious daily decisions that we have to make, and the better we make them, the better the results we will reap.

Easier said than done? Maybe, but there are some real practical things we can do each day to get in a routine so we can start helping ourselves to be the best we can be each and every day. Keep CDs or tapes in your car that are upbeat and positive. Personally, I listen to a lot of contemporary gospel and Christian music. If you are filling your mind, and it may even be our subconscious mind since a lot of the time we are only half listening to the song that is playing, with songs about violence, hate, cheating, lying, we should expect not to be at our emotional best. Get into something uplifting and encouraging.

Even before you leave the house, read something positive, study the bible, have an old sit-com on TV. I think the news is catching on to the fact that we don't want to start our day off with a lot of negative bombarding. If you notice, it seems the morning news shows have a lot more general interest stories, and our local news even has about every 15 minutes someone out on location at a fun event that is going on in the community. Let's take control of our lives! Hey, if you need to, pick up the phone and call someone whom you can count on to give you an uplifting conversation. We all know people like that, just as we know there are some people we are scared to call because all we will hear about are the world's problems. Call that positive person, lift them up and let them do the same for you. Determine that each day you are going to be a positive influence for everyone that you come in contact with. If you are not good at paying people compliments, start practicing. Work at catching people doing something good, and then tell them about it. If for no other reason, do this for yourself. Get how it works? If you start having a positive attitude and impact on those around you, making them feel better, think how much more enjoyable they are going to be to be around. And, then in turn, how much fun your life will become because of it. It could really become quite a chain reaction. One person really can make a big difference!

It's all about knowing we can do it and encouraging others to feel the same way. Just like when we are going through some tough times, when we get through a difficult day, we know we can make it through another one. It is the same with someone in sales, they make a sale and it gives them the encouragement to go and make another one. Or the marathon runner, they get through a mile, and they know they can conquer the next one. It's a strategy too. When you are on mile seven, are you focused one the 26th and final mile of the marathon? No, you should be focused on mile eight.

Just like in sales, focus on closing the deals in your pipeline and bringing in new business, don't be overwhelmed with your annual numbers that have to be met by the end of the year. Those will fall into place as you reach your daily, weekly, monthly, and quarterly goals.

It's the same with life. Don't sit around wondering "how am I ever going to make it through this year?" Just realize you are going to be able to make it through the day, and the next day and so on, and the year will take care of itself.

CHAPTER 4

Rally Time

James 1:12

[12] Blessed is the man who perseveres under trial, because when he has stood the test, he will receive the crown of life that God has promised to those who love him.

One of the things that causes the most stress in life is "change". Any re-direction, anytime something gets thrown in our path to make us suddenly rethink what we are going to do next is bound to cause some stress. Isn't it great when those days, weeks or even months happen when everything seems to fall into place? Smooth sailing! We all love it. But would we ever really grow or learn without change? No. And we would probably be using our brain even less than we already do. Plus, don't we always get much more satisfaction when we are working on a project and we have to work through some unpredictable issues and then finally successfully complete it, rather than if it had just magically slipped into place from step one. You know, like putting together a new gas grill or bicycle. I think the people who write those assembly instructions must really want to help us grow and mature, and have a great feeling of self satisfaction when three weeks later we finally finish putting it together.

We don't know what is just around the corner for us in life. When the potential need to be listed for a bi-lateral (double) lung transplant was first presented to me, needless to say, it was pretty shocking. But, I was also very blessed to have a great doctor with a great "bedside manner". The way the news was delivered to me and described to me, couldn't have been better. It was discussed in such a way that really left me in a positive frame of mind about the situation and my future.

One of the ways that it was explained was that I would only go on the list once my lung function dropped to a certain level to qualify me as a candidate. I was not at the point yet, but I was being prepared for that day. I also found out that there would be an extensive evaluation in order to be considered a viable candidate.

Now, the other thing that was explained to me was that when and if I was listed for a transplant, if my health did level out or even improve some, I would be put in an inactive status. Meaning, I would only move forward with the surgery if I, and my doctors, felt it was necessary at that time. That gave me a good feeling. I had all my bases covered.

I ended up being officially listed in August of 1997. I actually got a phone call on the afternoon of my 31st birthday. I was on my way out the door for dinner when the phone rang. I was told that my last lung function tests had taken a substantial drop and definitely had me in the range where I should be listed for transplantation. I would be listed to receive two new lungs. Both single lung and double lung transplants are done. In my case however, with always dealing with the chronic lung infections, it would be necessary for me to receive two new lungs. Otherwise, if I just received one new lung, my old lung would more than likely cause the new one to get infected. So, once I got off this phone call, everything started feeling a lot more real and the whole transplant process really started to sink in to me.

But, part of me really just went on with my life, and thinking that this would not happen for a long time. I guess I felt my health would improve and I wouldn't need the surgery. I also felt, and definitely believe, that God was in control of the situation and the outcome was in His hands.

I love the line from a song that talks about storms in our life, "Sometimes 'He' calms the storms, and sometimes 'He' calms His child". Meaning that sometimes God chooses to fix our problems (stopping the storm in our life) and other times He holds us close and comforts us during our hard times, allowing us also to grow and learn from them.

I was just talking to someone the other day who was facing a difficult time finding a new job after his company downsized. He was getting very anxious and frustrated, as well as losing patience. One of the things I said to him was to remember what he was going through now so he'd be able to use it someday to help someone else who was going through the same thing.

I had no idea all the great doors that were going to open for me by going through my transplant surgery. How much I would change as a person. My attitude, my strength, faith, knowledge, and most of all my appreciation for life and what we all truly have been given to live for each and every day.

When we are right in the middle of a difficult situation, that is always the hardest time to see any "positive" around us. I always think of it as if we were stuck down in a dark hole, like in a deep well. And we just can't see the way out. We know there is a bright light waiting for us at the top, but we are just too deep to be able to grasp on to it or have hope that it is there. But, as we begin to find a way to climb out of the well, we start to feel some encouragement. Initially we have to take the first steps to get things started in the right direction. We have to start to climb, we can't just wait for someone to come along and lift us up. We start to climb out and we start to see a glimmer of light, and a hope starts to lift our spirit, we can feel our attitude and excitement grow. And that light always looks better to us when we have not seen it in a while. Just like when a week or so goes by and it has been cloudy outside. We haven't seen the sun in several days. Once the sun finally appears, everyone's mood seems to change for the better. Everyone appreciates a sunny day much more when clouds have surrounded us for a long time.

It's like that when we experience some type of victory in life. Maybe it is a competition or sporting event that we are involved with. Think about those times that two teams are playing against each other, or two individuals are competing against each other in some type of event. Let's say we are watching something like this on TV, and one team or individual is dominating the other. What usually happens? We get bored with it and change the channel or leave. Kind of like when you are at a baseball game and one team is leading by 7 or 8 runs, it's a blowout. Everyone stands at the seventh inning stretch, and about half leave the game. They figure they've seen enough; the excitement of the game is over. Now compare that to an event that is neck and neck all the way down to the wire. No one changes the channel; no one heads to his or her car early. Everyone is on the edge of his or her seat. They want to see the strategy that is played out. They want to see how the coach calls the plays, how will the competitors position themselves to have the best possible finish. Not only are we excited to see the outcome, we are learning from this kind of process. Learning how those who are competing overcome their challengers. Just like each of us, in life, we can learn from our life challenges. It's the close calls, the challenges that we can develop skills from and understand better how to handle these situations the next time they come up and we can help those around us that may be going through this same type of thing. Think about what makes a great coach or player? They always talk about when a team goes to the Super Bowl or World Series, how many players are rookies vs. veterans. It's the veterans that know how to react in the pressure situations and have learned from previous experiences, and are expected to pull through when the going gets tough. We shouldn't get too upset when we face tough times in life, there is good that is going to come from it. We will become a veteran and a good coach as we develop a good game plan to make the most out of life and how to handle the next situation that comes up.

Look at it like this too. I love watching the "March

Madness" NCAA basketball games. It's almost guaranteed that there will be 'one point games' and overtime games. There are always the run-away blowouts too. Next time you are watching a game, notice the difference in the fans and the players, and the difference in how they react at the end of a game in those two types of situations. The team who just runs away with the win, leads the entire game, and posts a twenty-point victory, is that team happy? Sure. They celebrate.

But, now look at the team that was down by ten or fifteen points most of the game, then they get a spark of energy and start to come back in the last couple of minutes. The next thing you know it's an eight-point game, with one minute left. Then they cut it to four points and 45 seconds are on the clock. OK, no one is leaving the room, the coach is using all the timeouts perfectly, and you can see the nervousness on the faces of all the players. Even the referees have a heightened level of attention and excitement. The team that was down steals the ball and makes a three point shot, suddenly a team that was down by fifteen, is now within one point and only 20 seconds left on the clock. There is a foul, the winning team goes to the line and misses, and the underdog team gets the ball, 10 seconds on the clock, everyone in the gym, and at home, is on their feet! They dribble over the half court line, 7 seconds left, they drive in and take a shot with 4 seconds left, they miss, 2 seconds left, and the 6'8" center jumps up and tips in the rebound and wins the game as the buzzer sounds. OK, now that team is going to go crazy with excitement. They will all be out on the floor going wild. The crowd, not one of them had left early, will be in a state of shock. Why? Because they overcame the challenge, they did not give up, pushed themselves to the limit, and overcame adversity. Both teams are going to learn from the experience. And, yes, it could have gone either way, just like in our life situations. But we have to keep our eyes on our goal, and when the situation turns out for the better, we are going to have even a higher sense of satisfaction because we made it through the pain and came out a winner. Just like in baseball, there is nothing better than a home run in the bottom of the ninth to win the game. But remember, for this to happen, there can be no giving up or throwing in the towel. You have to keep yourself in the game and keep trying to make your dreams come true.

Think about it like this, a fireman goes to work one day, no alarms, no fires, and a quiet day. When he gets home, everything is fine, just another day. Let's say a different day, things go crazy, 2 fires and he's called out to a heart attack victim. The fires are successfully taken care of, and he saves someone's life by starting their heart again with CPR. Which day do you think he'd rather go through? All depends on the type of person they are, I guess? Some people want to cruise through life, some love the challenges. They know they learn from them, become a better person, and at the end of the day, they have a much higher sense of satisfaction and celebration. They thrive on that chance to rally back and end up on top!

CHAPTER 5

"A Plan For You"

Jeremiah 29:11

[11] For I know the plans I have for you," declares the LORD, "plans to prosper you and not to harm you, plans to give you hope and a future.

A story that always comes back to my mind when I am confused or frustrated about how a certain situation is turning out in my life, is something that happened to my brother, Rick, a long time ago. He was probably only seven or eight years old. It was after church one Sunday night and it was Rick's birthday. The big deal back then for kids was the Ronald McDonald party room at McDonalds. We had not even had a McDonalds for very long in our small town. And I always remember, every time we would go there we would stick our heads up against the window at the Ronald room, just so we could see the lucky kids who were getting to have a party. It was pretty cool, because you didn't have to sit out with the rest of the people in the restaurant; you had your own private area. Well, that night, my parents had a surprise party all planned for Rick. A bunch of his friends were going on ahead of us to be there before we arrived. He had no idea. Now, here's where this all gets good. We get in the car after church, all is going as planned, and his friends are on their way to McDonalds. But Rick had a craving for Dairy Queen. He knew we were going out to eat for his birthday, and it only made sense to him that he should get to pick where we went to eat. After all, it was his birthday. And, he was very convincing to us. He had even seen a new DQ commercial, and there was a new dessert treat out and what better time for him to get to try it, than his birthday? Little did he know that the DQ idea didn't even compare to what my mom and dad had in store for him. Isn't that just the way we are a lot of times in life? We are just convinced that we know what is best for us. And, many times we become so stubborn to change; we may miss out on a great opportunity in life. Well, we convinced Rick to go to McDonalds. Of course, he was not too happy the rest of the ride to get there.

But, imagine his surprise when he walked in and saw the Ronald McDonald room in all its beauty and splendor in his eyes. He'd never been in the room before, just seen it from the window. All his friends were waiting for him. His special birthday cake, which I am sure, was looking much better to him at that time than the DQ treat he was dreaming of. How could he ever have imagined that this was in store for him? If he had gotten his way, he would have missed out on all this. Something he had dreamed of for a long time. He really had himself convinced that his plan for himself was the best thing. And that nothing else could have compared to that. He probably had a hard time believing that we had his best interest in mind when we were trying to convince him to do what we wanted. Well, you can imagine his gratitude to mom and dad, not only for planning all this, but also for not giving into him and letting him change the plans. And I know my mom and dad, if his temper would have gotten out of control for not getting his way, we would have ended up at Dairy Queen, and I am sure they would have pointed out to him on the way there that all his friends were sitting in the "party room" waiting for him. That would have taught him a good lesson, and as a big brother, I am sure I would have gotten a kick out of it. But, Rick has always been easy going, and he went along with their plans instead of his, and he reaped the rewards because of it. What was his best plan for himself didn't even compare to what a caring father and mother had in store.

I have found myself feeling like that many times in my life. What I felt for sure was the best thing in my life did not even compare to what God had in store. Just as it was my parent's love and concern for my brother that their decisions were based upon, it is the same with our heavenly Father. His concern for us is always more than what we have for ourselves or could imagine for ourselves. Just like with my transplant situation, I sure felt that going through the surgery was not going to be the best thing for me. But looking back I can see so many things that have come about because of it, things that never would have otherwise. If my health had stabilized, if there was a miraculous healing, I know I would have been grateful; but still there were things that could have only happened to me, and specific experiences that I could have learned from, that only have happened because of the specific journey I was on. There have been people I have met, doors that have been opened up for me, and things that I have been able to get involved in and take part in that never would have happened otherwise. I had the DQ treat in my mind for myself, but God has given me the ultimate party room experience. And it has been and continues to be a great ride. There is no question that the few years since my transplant, have been more fulfilling than all the other 32 years prior to my transplant combined.

Look at this example. I was in a sales training seminar once. The trainer told a personal story that he had gone through.

He found himself out of work and looking for the next career opportunity in his life. He went on interview after interview, not sure why, for various reasons, the opportunities did not pan out. Then one day he entered in an interview process, and this seemed like the dream job of a lifetime. The company was going to relocate him, right where he and his wife wanted to be, it was the town where their families resided. The position was structured exactly for what his background had prepared him for. The compensation was better than what he had been used to. Perfect in every way. He said he prayed and prayed for this to work out, and as the interview process moved along, things just looked better and the company gave him many signs that he was the one for the job. Finally in the last interview they said they would be mailing him an offer in a week. He was ecstatic! But the offer did not come. So he called and found out that at the last minute they were made aware of someone whose background was a little more closely in line with their particular industry, and they made that person an offer. He was devastated.

Within a month, he was introduced to another company that he also very much liked, and was brought on with them.

He closed the story by saying, "that first company that I was sure was perfect for me, their name was The Enron Corporation."

CHAPTER 6

In Life's Waiting Room

Psalm 27:14

[14] Wait patiently for the LORD. Be brave and courageous.
Yes, wait patiently for the LORD.

Being on a transplant list was an emotional roller coaster. Really, just like any experience in life, with lots of ups and downs. A friend of mine always likes to say, "when you are going through a tough time, listen for that 'click, click, click' sound. That is the sound we hear when we are at the bottom of the roller coaster, and when it starts to go back up a hill, nice and slow, you hear that 'click, click' sound, then we know we will have our hands up in the air going for the ride of our life soon! Things will always get better."

I was on the transplant waiting list for 20 months. Fortunately, I was able to work the first 12 months of that time. That helped me keep myself, and my mind, occupied. But I found I was really pushing myself too hard. I really wanted to be able to just work right up until I was called or paged to go into my surgery. I had an office/desk job, so I felt it might be possible. But my lung functions kept dropping. Getting from my car into the office was becoming a real struggle; I really dreaded getting out of the car to head into work. To me, it may as well been climbing up a mountain or going up about 20 flights of stairs. I had to literally stop 6 or 7 times from the parking garage to the office suite. And I would always stop a final time in the restroom right outside my office to try and catch my breath so my co-workers would not see me so short of breath when I walked into work. I was on the phone a great deal for my job, and it was even very difficult to keep from getting short of breath while talking to my customers and clients. I remember one day, I had been at my desk for a while, and the person I was talking to asked if

I had just run across the office to answer the phone because I sounded as if I was trying to catch my breath. I had no idea it was that noticeable.

As hard as it was to give in, (I believe there is a difference between giving up and giving in) I knew I needed to take a medical leave from work. My doctors were also suggesting it in order for me to keep my strength up for the surgery. I knew it was the best thing to do. I needed to focus on my task at hand, and make sure I was as in as good of shape as possible for my surgery. This is kind of ironic, in the sense that my health was the worst it had ever been, so it was hard for me to think of getting myself in shape. But it was going to be more of a situation to try and maintain what I had, and not let myself slip anymore. The other piece of all this was that I had no idea how long I was going to be on the waiting list, no idea at all. Or, would I even get called? I really had to put myself in to a mindset that this could be a long process of needing to keep myself stable.

Unfortunately, there was a lot of "stuff" going on in my life all at the same time. Sometimes I actually think that might have been a blessing, having multiple issues to deal with. It seemed to keep my mind off any one issue for too long. Each acted as a distraction to the other.

I was going through a marriage separation, which led to divorce. All of this happened during the same 20-month waiting period for my surgery. I dealt with selling a home, needing to quit work, moving, and was also diagnosed with diabetes all during this same time. Like I said, with everything going on I really was not able to focus too heavily on any one issue at a time

I moved back in with my parents after needing to stop work. This was my second move in 6 months. Believe me, being in your early 30s, in a career, and married, and then needing to move back in with your parents, was never the plan that I had for myself, and I am sure it was not in my parents plans either. But, I sure was fortunate that I had them close by, and that we were such a close family and such good friends with each other. I was getting to the point that I was feeling so weak, I know I couldn't live on my own. I couldn't grocery shop, or run any errands like that without being extremely short of breath and exhausted.

One day I will never forget, I had asked my dad to take me out to the driving range. I still had a passion for golf. My plan was that I would just go out and hit golf balls everyday, even if for a few minutes at a time. I needed something fun to do and something to keep myself occupied. I knew my dad would carry my clubs for me. Walking was extremely hard. Walking and carrying something, regardless of the weight, was out of the question. But, I figured, I surely could just stand in one place, and swing a golf club. How much energy could that take? I had not been able to actually play golf in a long time, even with a cart, because just the walking to and from the cart to the tee box or green left me wiped out. But, I was going to give this a try at the range. Well, after about two swings, I felt like I had just sprinted a couple hundred yards. It left me panting for breath and light headed. So, we left the golf balls on the ground and headed back to the car. I remember that afternoon was one of my lowest points. I let myself get pretty bummed out. I was thinking, no relationship, no work, no golf, and no sweet foods with the diabetes news (at least I knew I really needed to watch how much of the 'good junk food' I ate). And, as much as I love my parents, they knew and wished I had my own place too. Don't get me wrong, they wanted their favorite son there (just kidding, Rick), but they wanted the best for me too, and they knew I wanted to be out on my own and feeling good enough to enjoy life.

I remember after returning from the driving range, my mom asked, "Why back so soon?" I know she knew all the frustrations I was feeling when I told her I was not able to swing a golf club anymore.

She knew all the things that I felt were piling up on me, and she looked me in the eye and said, and I will never forget this, "your day will come, these tough times will not last forever". I really needed to hear that. We all need to be better at encouraging each other like that. I've heard people say, "well, don't encourage them, you don't know if things will get better". But, what my mom said to me was a form of instilling hope. She was not making me some sort of a lifetime promise, that I was going to hold her to. It was not a promise that I was going to live forever and never have any problems here on earth again. She was telling me what she wanted for me and what she hoped for me in my life. If we think about it, things can always get better. But, in order to do so, it will have to start with our faith and attitude being in line. I felt lifted up inside when she gave me those words. So, in a sense, I was already better off with my situation. I was starting to focus on the positive around me instead of focusing on all the other "stuff" that was happening. And, I didn't want to dwell on the negative anyway; I just needed a push in the right direction. Someone might say I didn't even know if I was going to live through all this. And that's correct. A lot of days I was not sure if I was going to make it until the next day or not. At this stage, just getting into bed and pulling the covers up, left me gasping for air for several minutes. Many nights I wondered if my breathing was ever going to settle down and if I would be waking up the next morning or not.

I learned a very valuable lesson from a minister from my church. He and his wife were in a head on car collision, one that after seeing pictures of their car, everyone was surprised that they made it out alive. He said that he had so many people telling him, "you were so lucky, you could have died.

That would have been terrible!" He said he appreciated the concern but he got tired of people telling him how terrible it would have been if he had died. He said what good is our faith if we go around feeling that the worst thing that could happen to us is die. Now, don't get him wrong, he wants to live, and live a long healthy life here, but he also knows that when his time comes, that he will have an eternity with no pain and suffering. Putting your life and trust in Christ, and giving your life to Him, not only gives you the strength to rely on each day that we are on earth, it is also the best life insurance policy available, and it lasts forever.

It is probably rare these days that there is no stress at all in our lives, rarely even does a day go by that we don't have some stress to deal with. And, of course, some days it just seems like every hour is full of stress. We've all had days where we didn't even feel like we wanted to be around anyone, or even get out of bed to start our day. There have been times when I was planning a speaking event, and my goal is really to encourage others and motivate them into positive action. Then, all the sudden, a "big chunk of stress" would creep into my life. My first thought was, "how can I get up in front of a large crowd, and convey a positive image with all this going on in my life?" Or, even worse, would think I needed to change around the material I was going to present because I didn't think I was in a good enough mood to talk about all the great things I had to share with my audience. Why? Because something had frustrated me or was worrying me. Something was trying to take the fun and excitement out of what I was about to talk about. I quickly learned that we have to separate ourselves from our stress. Sure, some things we have to deal with. Sometimes it is a part of our life; sometimes it's because of our job, our education, parenting, or the many other things that could be going on, health, relationships, finances. But it does not mean we have to let it consume us, or focus on it

24 hours a day. We can't let it ruin our day, or ruin us from keeping our sight on all the great things we have going on. Sometimes I really think we feel like everything has to go perfectly in our lives for us to be happy. I've heard it said that 95% of everything that is going on in our life is good, and about 5% would be considered not so good. Why is it that we tend to focus on the 5%?

Think about the businessman or businesswoman who has a bad day at work. When they come home, it seems the day will flow over right into what ever they had planned for the evening and make that miserable too. Instead, why can't it become a natural practice that once we walk in the door at home we see all the "positive" around us, and put the rest of the day behind us? When you walk into your home to your spouse and your children you have an evening to spend together. Make the most out of that; enjoy that time to the fullest. Put all the other things that cluttered up your day behind you so you can focus on the good, your family.

Look at it like this. Ever drive down a road full of speed bumps, and you found out that you could swing around the edge of them to miss them? It didn't mean they were going away, they were still there, but you were able to smooth out your ride, and enjoy it more. And, you didn't need to be getting that constant jarring feeling of bouncing your insides around, which of course is not good for you or your car.

My point here is, let's try not to miss out on the great things in life just because we have to deal with some bumps. Just like in the car, eventually we will have to get back over in the lane with the bumps, and that's fine. We just have to remember there will always be smooth roads ahead again.

We have got to learn to give it our best shot. We can't just sit around and expect great things to happen. Or for that fact, we can't just sit around and expect anything at all to happen.

We have to make things happen. Have faith, make it happen. Get into the game and get things started and into action.

Sometimes we have to bring things down to our level to understand them better. If parents wanted their children to have a good education, they would take them to get registered, give the kids a ride to school or arrange for the bus to pick them up, get books ordered, school supplies, and even help with homework at night. That's a lot of help. Now, what if the children decided each day when they were dropped off at the front door of the school, they were just going to sit by the door all day and wait to be picked up that afternoon. And they never even went into a classroom. The parents did all they could, but there was no effort on the kid's part.

I think that is sometimes the way we are with our faith and God. We expect things to happen, but we are not putting in the effort on our part. Just as our earthly parents want us to grow and learn, our Heavenly Father wants us to take action to help ourselves too. I know a lot of times we've been given an opportunity, a talent, a skill, but we are not making the most of it. It's going to take some work on our part. No one is going to do the work for us. Nor do I think we would want it that way. We will get much more satisfaction when we see the rewards from our efforts. And remember, if it was easy to accomplish what we wanted to, everyone would be doing it. Writing a book is not easy for me. I read once that at some point almost everyone has had a feeling they would like to write a book, about 80% decide not to do it. I'm glad everything I have tried in life is not easy or I'd never have a chance to win. Just the ones willing to put in the extra effort and work are going to win.

You might think this, why should I put in the effort, I just don't feel that I can compete with those who are in: the same sport as me, same type of business that I am in, the same major I chose in school. They are all working so hard, I don't think I can keep up, so I will just try and get by.

Bad choice and wrong too.

Listen, I wish there was an accurate way that someone could get a statistic on how many people really apply themselves to accomplish their goals.

I have been in the recruiting business for many years, and am amazed at the lack of effort some people will put forth. I have seen people who were out of work, needing a job, or at least they are saying they need a job, and then they take a week or two to get a resume submitted. How can you be that busy, especially when you are not working? But, I guess that is good news for the aggressive types, because that is your competition and you will have no problem passing them by!

I love the old joke about the newlywed couple. One was a very prim and proper type, always handed everything they needed. One day the mother-in-law was over at the house. The newly married young adult pointed out a stain in the kitchen sink, and just couldn't figure out how it had gotten there and didn't think it would ever go away. The mother-in-law kindly gave some advice not to worry about it, and to just try a little 'elbow grease' and it would come right out. She said that always takes care of everything. Later that night the newly weds were talking and the one mentioned what they had learned from the mother-in-law. They had just one question for their new spouse, "Where can I find 'elbow grease?" The other said; "if I were you, I wouldn't worry about looking for it; I don't think you will ever find any".

So, be patient during these tough times, stay focused, keep plugging away, and you will get to where you want to be.

CHAPTER 7

The Call

Isaiah 40:29

[29] He gives power to those who are tired and worn out; he offers strength to the weak.

My roller coaster ride continued while on the waiting list for my transplant. We always hear on the news how we don't want to 'over use' antibiotics or our body could become resistant to them. Well, that happened to me. All my life, since 10, I had no choice but to be taking them daily due to all the lung infections. It was a real on-going battle to fight these respiratory flare-ups.

While I was on the transplant waiting list, some tests came back that the medications that I had been using most of my life to keep me healthy now had basically become useless to me. Although it seemed they were still having some positive effect on me, medically speaking and from the test results, my body had reached a level of resistance that the medications would not work in a serious infection situation. This meant I had to be put in an inactive status on the transplant list. The reason for this was it would not be practical to take someone through a surgery such as this without having an option to administer antibiotics if needed. So, I was immediately taken off these medications that I had been counting on to help keep me from getting sick for over twenty years. The hope was to let my body build up 'sensitivity' again. This was a challenge, because I could tell a difference right away. The small effect they did still have for me seemed to be very noticeable given that my overall state of health was now very low and I was needing any help I could get. But, I knew this is what I had to do in order to reach my long-term goal of being in the best possible shape for my transplant surgery.

We often have to do that in life, we have to give up some short-term benefit to make our long-term goals. I was listening to a financial advisor give a presentation on positioning yourself in the best financial position. He made a great comment that I think goes along with many aspects of our life. He was talking about debt, and said the best thing we can do for ourselves, is to get ourselves out of debt. He said it is not going to be fun going through this process, because there will be some things that have to be given up, but when you get to that stage, debt free, that is when you will have an overall greater satisfaction in life and a situation of being much more stress free. Then you will really enjoy more what you have.

Well, this is what I needed to do in my health situation; I needed to suffer through some short-term trials in order to get myself primed for a chance to receive a transplant. I had to do this by staying in very close contact with my doctors. I needed to be able to let them know how I was feeling and if I felt myself starting to go down hill. If that were the case, they would try to find some combination of medication that would still work against the organisms in my body, something that could get me to a stable base line. But, I knew the downfall would be that it would also reduce any sensitivity that I had regained. So, it was a real battle and tough decisions had to be made almost on a daily basis. I wanted to hold out as much as I could, but I also could not take a chance of getting very ill and too far down so that I would not being able to recover. I learned from going through that experience, and really appreciated the relationship my doctors and I developed.

Well, the wait still continued. I had now been listed for nearly a year and a half. Once the transplant center felt I was getting close to the top of the list in January of 1999, they put me through a final orientation. Of course, there was still no way of knowing when I might receive "the call", or if I would ever receive it. I remember that conversation so well at my doctor appointment in January.

I had been asked to be in one of my best friend's wedding as a groomsman. Funny, this was all getting in such a serious stage for my transplant, and I wanted to know what my doctor thought my chances would be to be able to accept the offer to be a groomsman for this wedding that was six months away. I think this was a way to try and keep myself distracted from what all was going on and try to focus on other things in life. The doctor said I could be called in a week or a year or even longer. It was so hard to tell. I knew I couldn't walk down an aisle in the condition I was in then, and the only way I was going to be able to participate in my friends wedding was if I was through the surgery and in a successful recovery mode.

My doctor asked me if I was ready to go through the final activation, I remember asking what other options I had. He said if I wanted to wait a couple of months... maybe I needed to take care of some things in my life before being at a final stage to go through a major surgery, he said I could for sure do that. I asked him what he thought, and he reminded me how low my lung functions had dropped and that I did not have much of a cushion before I was basically at a zero lung function, and we both knew what that meant. I said I didn't have anything to wait around for; I was ready to get things going. I had already been through a very detailed evaluation when I was first listed, so this was a final activation process. I was given a pager and was now on call all the time. I was surprised how many wrong numbers could be dialed into a pager. I remember the first time it went off it was quite a shock. Once, early in the morning, I was still sleeping and the pager was on my dresser. It was a real jolt of a wake up call. The pager was really a back up to my home phone. The protocol then was to call the home phone first, and if for some reason the transplant team could not get through or if I was not at home, the pager would be called. So, when the pager went off, even though I was home, I still wondered if maybe they had tried my home phone and this was "the call". Also, at this stage, I was rarely leaving my house; I didn't feel well enough to be out much at all.

Well, the telephone ringing had really taken on a whole new meaning for me too, especially when it would ring at an hour that we didn't usually get a phone call. Every time it would ring, it gave me a unique feeling, a feeling of excitement combined with a 'knot in my stomach.' Strangely enough, with all the times I had been in the hospital, I had never had any kind of major surgery, really, not any type of surgery at all to speak of. So, this being my first experience, and now it was going to come basically out of the blue. Each day was definitely filled with anticipation.

I remember April 8th, 1999 very well. I was not feeling well at all that day. Even worse than what had gotten to be "normal" for me. In fact, I thought I was getting the flu or something too. I was having a lot of trouble sleeping, so I decided to just stay up late and watch TV. I was watching all the late-night comedy talk shows. I went to bed around 1:30 in the morning, which was now April 9th. And I remember lying in bed just watching the alarm clock. I know I saw it turn over to 4AM before I fell asleep. I had also turned off the ringer on my phone, I was hoping I could get some sleep in the morning, and since my dad worked out of the home, the phone would ring early sometimes. Well, at 4:45 AM, my dad came to the doorway of my bedroom and announced to me that I had a phone call. I, of course, had not heard the phone ring. I don't know about you, but I am not used to getting many phone calls at that hour. The first thing I did was to turn up my oxygen. And, the voice on the other end of the phone told me that new lungs had been located for me and I was to head down to the hospital. Well, this was it. I will never forget that morning. The mixture of emotions was amazing.

We started making some quick phone calls. I called my

brother first thing, and then we made the rest of the calls from the cell phone on the way. We called our minister, other people from the church, family, and friends. I think I was on the phone most of the way to the hospital, about a 40 minute drive, probably a little less that morning. Hopefully the police would have understood if we had gotten pulled over! Also, having those phone calls to make helped keep me calm. We were at the hospital by 6AM. My dad dropped my mom and me off right at the door. We grabbed a wheel chair, put the oxygen tank on the chair, and headed to the floor where I was to report. Dad was close behind after he got the car parked. My oxygen tank fell off just as we made the first turn down a hallway. There was an older gentleman walking by, and he immediately came over to help us. I will never forget that. I am sure he has forgotten it by now, but it was a nice relief to me to have someone willing to reach out and help us at 6AM, it sure made a big impact on me. We got off the elevator and headed to the nurses' station. This was amazing. Before we even said a word, or told them who I was; a nurse looked at me with a big smile and said, "You must be Randy Sims?" Her smile got even bigger as she said, "We've been waiting for you and are all ready to help you get settled in". OK, Wow. I think they even congratulated me for being there, and all of the sudden I felt like some kind of a celebrity. Whoever that person was, she had a real gift. She gave my emotions an amazing boost and jump-started my attitude, something that I needed desperately that morning.

Plus, the nursing staff was not nervous about this; in fact they were excited that I was there. They made me feel like this was just the best thing that had happened to them all year. And you know what, their attitude started to rub off on me. Amazing how that works, isn't it? And, in fact, every person that was put in my path that morning was in a good mood, happy, and even had a great sense of humor. Boy, I thanked

God I did not get a bunch of crabby people who didn't like being up at 6AM assigned to me. These attitudes that were surrounding me were terrific.

Then, I had some news delivered to me that I was not expecting. They were checking my vital signs and found I was running a fever. Not good. They thought it might be at a level that would not allow me to be able to go into surgery and immediately got on the phone with the doctors and surgery staff. They checked it all out, and it was determined that it was a level that was considered safe. I was realizing how fortunate I was that everything was falling into place and I was going to be able to get this surgery that I desperately needed to save my life.

Then, I was given more news. I was told I might be getting sent home. It seemed the process had slowed down for some reason. The team of surgeons that went out to retrieve the organs had not left yet. So, it was thought that there was some last minute discovery and that maybe the lungs were determined not to be able to be used for transplant?

This was explained to me in my orientation. It was called a "dry run". Everything has to be perfect, so many things timed just right, at any stage of the process, in all the double checks, something can be discovered to cause it to be necessary to call off the surgery. It was of course necessary to have me at the hospital once a donor was located, and then I would have to wait to see if the all the processes fell into place. There are so many details it really is amazing. There are so many people involved: doctors, surgeons, nurses, lab technicians, pilots, ambulance drivers, operating room technicians, anesthesiologists, patient transporters, and of course, the family of the donor, who I will make an attempt, later in this book, to express my gratitude to. So, I sat in my hospital bed and waited. I made more phone calls. Would I be going home, back in my regular routine, or was this miracle going to really happen for me?

It was around 9AM, when my brother got there. He had about a 3-hour drive from where he lived. The first words out of his mouth when he walked in the room were "well, it's a go!" My words to him were "what are you talking about?" I thought maybe he had just ordered breakfast for us, or something (of course I was not allowed to eat)? He explained that when he walked by the nurse's station, they had said, "You must be Randy's brother?" We do look a lot alike. He told them yes and they mentioned they were just about to go to my room and let me know that they just received a call and that my surgery was on, so they let him deliver the news to me. That was pretty neat.

Things started moving quickly then. I had to put on those white panty hose things, you know, they look like support hose. But they are necessary to help protect from blood clots in the surgery. Let me think: white hosiery, a hospital gown, and I think even a hair net, yip, I was looking good. The bad part was, I was so short of breath; I couldn't even get those stocking things on myself. I needed help. My brother was in the room with me and he helped me. All those times of me picking on my little brother, doing the natural big brother thing, I was afraid that was all going to come back to haunt me. I could just see him tying one end of the stocking to my IV pole. But, I guess even brothers can have a serious moment from time to time.

Next I was taken down to the holding room, which was just outside the operating room. It was just amazing all the things that were going on around me, and hard to believe that I was the center of attention. There were constant phone calls from the surgery retrieval team to the hospital staff in the holding room. They were taking me through, step by step, starting all the necessary IV lines to have me ready for surgery. The calls with the updates kept coming in from the team of surgeons. I was later told that once my new lungs were in the process of transport, the pilots and surgeons on the plane kept in constant phone and radio contact with the operating staff that was about to work on me, right up until the time they got to operating room.

We had a very special time of prayer before I went into the operating room. And I remember asking my family to, please, not worry about me. I was going to be asleep anyway, and it sure didn't seem fair for them to be worrying all that time.

I was still kidding around and joking with the O.R. team, who was prepping me, right up until the time they put me to sleep. Having all these people around me with a good sense of humor was great. It was exactly what I needed to help keep me calm. As a matter of fact, I was still telling stories right up until the time they put me to sleep. I think I had a little nervous energy going, and putting me to sleep was probably the only way they could get me to shut up. Everything was timed so precisely, I remember the last thing I heard was, OK, it is 1:32 PM, and we needed to have you asleep by 1:30, so start breathing into this mask. I saw a lot of stainless steel around me. I remember thinking, wow; it is absolutely amazing what is going to be happening to me while I am sleeping. And, if this all goes well, I will wake up with a clear, scar-free set of lungs, something I had not felt in a long, long time. Then I dozed off to a sound sleep

My family had told me that they were getting constant updates from the operating room. I know that was a big help to them. They also said that the waiting room filled up with friends and family members stopping in to check how things were going. That was a big help to keep them occupied. It was a long day for them, about 7 or 8 hours of surgery, and then, of course, recovery. I was told that the first time I started waking up and acknowledging those around me was around 11:30 that night. I started immediately writing notes (I had breathing tubes in my mouth). The first thing I wrote was "did the surgery actually happen or not?" I definitely did not feel any pain and wondered if it all actually happened? The next thing I wrote had something to do with what was going to happen as far as dinner plans. I think the medications were kicking in. Believe it or not, I had remembered my mom was planning a big family dinner for us over the weekend. And I was looking forward to that roast dinner. So, I wanted to know what happened to that roast. The notes kept going; I asked if I could have a grape snow cone. Of course that was out of the question. Then, the next day, Saturday, around noon, the breathing tubes came out. Wow. What a feeling. It was great, a real miracle. It was the first deep, clear, breath that I have felt in a long time. It was the most enjoyable and amazing feeling that I could have imagined.

It was also the most enjoyable hospital stay that I had ever had. Each day I felt better and stronger. Each day I could feel my breathing getting better and I was able to get off the oxygen and still not be short of breath when I walked down the hallway. It was truly amazing, just a few days before I was in a wheel chair and on oxygen 24 hours a day. Now, I was scheduling time to walk on the treadmill at the rehab center, with no oxygen. I used to dread getting on the treadmill, now I looked forward to it. And, I was really getting into the hospital food, even eating was easier, and it was much more enjoyable than before. I was in the hospital for ten days. Each day was better than the last. I felt better, I was seeing great improvements, and I loved the challenge of getting stronger each day. I had all kinds of great gifts and cards and visitors that kept me company. Having the strong support of those around me was very important to keep me mentally up-beat.

Many people have asked me what the specifics were like on the day of surgery and the days following.

Here are some entries from my journal:

April 9th

- Phone call from the hospital at 4:45am, new lungs had become available for me. (I was scared, excited, nervous and turning up my oxygen all at the same time)
- Arrive at the hospital 6:15am (I had been at that hospital 100+ times, of course this time I take the wrong turn down a hallway and got lost)
- Found the right floor 5 minutes later!
- Got in my room, now the wait begins...
- Go to the 2nd floor holding room outside the OR at 11am, the phone is ringing off the hook in there with updates and calls regarding my new lungs
- I am put under around 1pm.
- The new lungs arrived at 4:30pm. Right lung was the first to be taken out and replaced followed by the left lung.
- Surgeon went to the waiting room to give my family a report at 7:30pm
- Transferred to ICU at 8:30pm
- Start waking up around 11pm. Not sure what to think, just wanting to know if the surgery was a success

April 10th

- The breathing tubes (ventilator) came out at noon FIRST DEEP BREATH IN A LONG TIME, FELT GREAT!
- Sat up in a chair early that evening, hard to believe I was out of bed so fast. Not a lot to keep me occupied, so I started counting the number of tubes I had coming out of my body, I think it was 16 all together.

April 11th

- Walked around in my ICU room
- Transferred out of ICU to a regular hospital room 4pm

April 12th
- I was able to take off the oxygen tubes, kind of made me nervous to try and breathe without being connected to oxygen
- Walked down the hallway, no oxygen, and did not get short of breath
- It had been four days since I had any real food. That night I got to eat, and I was starving. "Hospital chicken and mashed potatoes" never tasted so good.

April 13th
- My first chest tube on the right side was taken out (note to self, use the morphine pump as much as possible before they take the next one out!)

April 14th
- First chest tube from my left side was removed (note to self, they actually tie a knot into your skin with the stitches just as soon as they pull it out, the more morphine the better)

April 16th
- 2nd chest tube removed from my left side
- I had not shaved in over a week and was starting to look like a cave man. One of the volunteers came in and helped me with that. Here I was at one of the best and most technological hospitals in the world, so I was not sure why they used one of those pink disposable razors to try and shave a week's worth of growth on my face. When the doctors did their rounds that afternoon, they were not sure if the cuts on my chest from surgery, or the new ones on face needed the most attention. But, it felt great to be clean-shaven.

Saturday April 17th

- All lab tests are coming back good
- The main central IV line that was in my neck was taken out, what a great feeling.
- Rick back in town to visit, he brought me in a pizza (I was starting to feel like a real person again, not sure how he was able to get the pizza in, but glad he did)

April 18th
- Final chest tube removed (I'm starting to get the hang of this now)

April 19th
- Walked 20 minutes on the treadmill, no oxygen needed. Most fun I've had exercising in a long time!
- Discharged, Sent home! Strange mixture emotions, as excited as I am to go home, a feeling that I will miss seeing those people on a daily basis who were a main part of this victory in my life. Also, a little nervous about being back in the real world after such a major surgery

April 20th
- Went to the hospital at 10am for my scheduled rehab. I walked .49 miles on the treadmill in 30 minutes.

April 21st
- Went to the hospital again for rehab., but was experiencing tremendous pain in my stomach. I had to be put in a wheel chair to get around. I thought those days were behind me. I was not able to get on the treadmill today, what a bummer. Instead many tests were run and I was sent home to wait on the results. 4:30 that afternoon my doctor's office called me and said I was going to need to be admitted immediately that my liver had shut down, and we had to figure out what was going on to cause this to happen. So, my parents rushed me to the hospital and I was admitted that night.

April 22nd

- Back in the hospital bed. No food allowed. Many tests were run, but no answers yet. The pain was more severe, much worse than anything I experienced during the transplant surgery.

April 23rd

- No food allowed still. But I felt too bad to be hungry. I was unable to sleep, my eyes were loosing focus, and it was even hard to get the energy to speak. I don't think I had ever felt this bad in my life. The one positive thing that I could focus on is that it felt so good to be able to breathe. That afternoon I was taken in for an exploratory surgery, and was told it was going to be a big risk, especially just coming out of a major surgery 2 weeks ago.
- Fortunately, they found the problem, and it was something that could be fixed during surgery. A valve near my liver had become blocked, and basically it was causing my body to poison itself. What a relief when it was repaired!

April 24th

- Broth and Jell-O diet, I'll take it!

April 25th

- Broth and a different flavor of Jell-O. And, my final lab work came back and that was my ticket home again.

Monday, April 26th

- Back to my regular daily rehab routine at the hospital. Treadmill, and exercises to build strength. Lots of lab tests too.
- Still only Broth and Jell-O diet

April 27th
- Graduated to soup!

April 28th
- 11am bronchoscope scheduled. (This is when they put tubes into the lungs to take biopsies and the doctors are able to view the inside of the lungs for any potential problems)

April 29th
- Walked .68 miles in 30 minutes, amazing to me that I could do that.

Wed. May 5th
- Staples (around 50) and stitches taken out of my chest, what a great feeling.

Wed. May 12th
- Tested positive for a common post transplant virus, IV lines needed to be started to treat this

Weekend of May 29/30th
- Rick in town to visit. Back to church for first time since my surgery. Went by a putting green to putt for the first time in months, walked around the mall for a while (had not done that in months either) Then we rented a movie. I will never take these things for granted again.

June 4th
- At the hospital for my normal rehab, exercise and follow-up. When I got on the elevator, there were a couple of guys wearing jump suits. They were pilots. They had been on a transport run for a transplant surgery. It was fascinating to get to talk to them. Understanding all they did on their end to make my process work. It just continues to amaze me how so many pieces have to

fall exactly into place on such short notice in order for everything to work the way it needs to.

Weekend of June 26/27th
- About thirteen weeks after my surgery, I was able to go to my friend's wedding, and I went out and celebrated that next day by playing my first nine holes of golf (in probably 2 years). Rick and I teed off at 10:37am. I shot a 45, he shot a 52. Not only did the surgery let me breathe again, I think if fixed my slice too.

Friday September 17th
- A little over 5 months post surgery; I was at the mortgage company, signing papers to close on my new home.

Monday October 11th
- Back to work. A six-month observation period was in order by the lung transplant center, to make sure everything was going well before being fully released. Never thought I could be so excited to walk into work.

It's amazing; I just kept feeling better and better. My parents were at the hospital each day; I could see the excitement on their face as I kept getting stronger, one day at a time.

I remember waking up one afternoon in the hospital and my dad was sitting in a chair near my bed. He had a big smile on his face. He told me he had been counting the number of breaths I was taking while sleeping. He told me then that there were many afternoons that I would fall asleep on the couch at their house, and he couldn't believe how fast and hard I would breath, even while sleeping. That it was obvious it was a real struggle. He was amazed at the difference and how much easier it was for me to sleep and breath.

CHAPTER 8

Using Your Abilities

2 Corinthians 9:6

⁶ Remember this: Whoever sows sparingly will also reap sparingly, and whoever sows generously will also reap generously.

You know, going through challenges of life is a lot like being in sales for a living. For those of you who have been in any type of sales, you know there are always going to be objections and rejections thrown at you, and you just have to figure out the best way to handle them. I have always tried to look at anything that was thrown at me in life, with an attitude of never giving up. And remember, there is a difference in "giving up" and "giving in", right? Many times we have to give in to certain situations that are out of our control. But, that does not mean we have to give up on making the best out of the situation. Do you see the difference? Just because you might be thrown a curve ball in life and you have to make some adjustments that you had not planned on, which in turn can result in giving in to the change, that does not mean that you have to give up on your our ultimate goal. Sometimes, it just means there needs to be some flexibility to have some redirection on your part. Before my transplant, I constantly needed to make adjustments, and give in to certain things that I necessarily did not want to. A lot of them were lifestyle adjustments. There were things that I would regularly discover that I could not physically do anymore. I was not giving up on my ultimate goal, but had to give in to the fact that I just couldn't do certain things. And, I had to realize that I needed to rely on people to help me with certain things too. In my case, it included things like going to the grocery store, or getting to and from the doctor's office, and even help with meals. So, I always tried to look at the big picture and make the best out of what I had going on, and try to enjoy it. Some of the best advice I was ever given regarding this came in the form of a prayer. A minister and good friend of mine prayed with me one day. I know he could tell my health was really going down hill, and that I was not doing well. I think he also sensed my need for encouragement. He prayed that day that God would show me some type of victory each day. Regardless of how big or small, that I would see something that would help me to be able to focus on a "positive" instead of being so overwhelmed with all the other "stuff" I had going on. It really worked and in many ways. But it also took some action on my part. I had to put in some effort on all this. Just like any good thing in life, we have to be willing to go after it. I started looking for the positive in my life to help keep me cheered up and more focused. The victories that I looked for, I was able to find in many forms. A card, an encouraging phone call, maybe I felt a little better than the day before, or at least for part of the day I felt not as bad. I tried to focus on this time that I was getting to spend with my family and making the most of it. It was not always easy, it was like anything else, something that had to be worked at, and given a concentrated effort. I found myself needing to take charge; we can't just sit around and wait for things to happen on their own.

I love the parable in the Bible about the talents. A master gave three servants talents. One was given five talents, one was given two talents, and the third servant was given one talent. A talent was a considerable amount of money. And I think it is beneficial for us to use the example, and look at talents not just as monetary, but also, the personal abilities we have been given. It is also important to note, that it states the talents were divided by each person's ability. So, the person who was given the most was deemed to have the ability to utilize this amount of 'talent'.

The servant who was given five talents immediately went to work, and put the talents to use, investing them wisely.

The servant given two talents did the same, and each of them doubled the money their master had given to them. But, the third servant became scared with what was given to him and he took it away and buried it. He did not want to risk what was given to him. He did not even try to use the talent he had. So, he never got to experience what the other two servants were able to experience. When the master came back, he was very pleased with the first two, but when he found out what had happened to the third servant, and that he had buried his single talent, he took it from him and gave it to the man who had doubled his to ten.

We all have special abilities. We have all been given special gifts. But it takes work and dedication to make things happen with them. It also takes being able to realize what we have and then determining the best ways to utilize it. Have you ever wondered how it is possible for someone who has a very obvious disability to overcome it and become exceptional in a specific area? Blind people who are wonderful musicians, people with physical disabilities who have become sports superstars, people who have overcome some type of tragedy and gone on to help others in some way. It almost seems like this would be impossible. But, they have been able to focus on their individual skills, abilities, and talents, and not on what others might consider a disadvantage. Was it easy for them to overcome their obstacles and reach these incredible levels of success? I would have to guess that it was not. But I bet each of them would do it all over again because of the satisfaction they received and how much more fulfilling their lives were because of it!

Anyone who wants to achieve, to go out and double their abilities rather than to bury them is going to have to take that first step. See, we've been given something, but we have to be the ones who develop it. It takes work and dedication to make things happen. We can't just sit around and wait for something to happen to us. We have to want it and go after it. It is about as simple as when we are young and want a new bicycle more than anything. Our parents can set a new bike in the driveway, but it is not going to do us a bit of good, or provide any pleasure to us if we don't get on it and ride it. We could sit there all day and think about it and look at it, but until we get on it and start peddling, we sure are not going to receive the fulfillment that was meant to come from it. So, get on the bike and start peddling and having fun in life!

It's the same when a child gets completely spoiled by their parents. Always getting everything they could ever want or need handed to them. How will that child be able to develop a work ethic? And even more important, how will they be able to develop the drive they need to get the most out of life?

You may say to yourself, not me, I don't have any special gifts. Well, that may be your first problem. What you are telling yourself could be a serious issue. Ever heard of "affirmations" or even more specifically, "positive affirmations"? It consists of saying something repeatedly to yourself, telling yourself something until you believe it.

Let's say you are a teacher, or a salesperson, or whatever your career, positive affirmations are very important. And, they are important in the non-career part of your life, too. Imagine you are on your way to work and keep saying to yourself all the way there "no way I am going to be able to keep those little brats under control today" (that could apply to you if you are a teacher or salesperson I guess) Maybe you also tell yourself that you don't feel well, you don't want to go to work and you don't really care much about how your day goes... Or, I am not up for this sales meeting, I don't feel like making a presentation, and the last thing I want to do is to start prospecting for new business this afternoon. Wow, what a sad way to start a day. We are not even giving ourselves a chance. Now, reverse it:

I am the best teacher.

I am excited to be able to have the chance to mold and develop children.

I am the top sales person, the best. I know I will be able to close my opportunities today, and will do it to help better my family and my company.

I am in business to help others, and I will do my best to leave a very positive impact on those around me.

I am fortunate and blessed to have this career, and I am going to make the most of it and give it my all.

Say these things out loud, and with a smile on your face. Don't worry about what the person in the car next to you is thinking when they look over and see you talking to yourself. Believe me, this will work. Just give it a try. Maybe you were brought up in a tough environment and had people around you always bringing you down and telling you "you could never be able to do that". Maybe you never had the encouragement you deserved. Well, do yourself a favor, start encouraging yourself, and do it every day. Don't just try this once or twice, start filling your mind with these things and saying these things to yourself every day. Start making yourself smile more, if you think that sounds crazy, just try it. I know I have. For whatever reason, your brain seems to know what shape your mouth is in, and it seems to do amazing things for your attitude. You have to believe in yourself in order for others to believe in you. That's why the best sales people always have a high level of confidence.

Can you imagine a counselor going into work and thinking "how can I help others when I have my own problems in my life to deal with?" Well you know what? We all have problems in our life. Let's face it. Unfortunately the world is full of problems. But it is also full of a lot of goodness and success. Remember, focus on the good, proclaim the positive through affirmations, and deal with the rest in your best possible attitude.

You will be amazed the difference it makes. My dad always tells me, why get worked up over things that you can't control in life, enjoy what's going on around you, and what you can't control will take care of itself anyway.

CHAPTER 9

Overcoming The Obstacles

James 1:2–4

2-4 Consider it a sheer gift, friends, when tests and challenges come at you from all sides. You know that under pressure, your faith-life is forced into the open and shows its true colors. So don't try to get out of anything prematurely. Let it do its work so you become mature and well-developed, not deficient in any way.

I love the old saying "Obstacles are just stepping stones on our way to success". You know, I believe that is completely true. In every situation that has presented an obstacle in our lives, we should be able to look back and see how we were able to grow and mature from it. It should have made us a stronger person and a better person. Those obstacles should also prepare us to better help others someday who might be going through the same or similar situations.

We have two definite paths that we can take when we hit one of these bumps in the road. And don't get me wrong; I know some of these things are not just a small or short-lasting bump. Someone could have grown up in an abusive situation or be in one at any stage of their life. And we know, when we are right in the middle of the crisis, it is the most difficult time to imagine ever getting out if it. It is just like being stuck in the center of a big crowd of people or in the middle of a traffic jam. We can see no way out until things start to move and we start to make our way to an opening. Then we can see some light at the end of the tunnel.

Ever been in a terrible traffic situation? You know, one where you actually put your car in park and everyone around you is getting out of his or her vehicles to visit with each other? You have no idea how long you will be stuck. You wonder if you even have enough gas to get you through. You start thinking about what will happen if you run out of gas, and, you think about all the things that this will interrupt that you have scheduled for that day or evening. If you don't have a cell phone with you, you start to worry about the people who were expecting you to be at a certain place at a certain time. Then suddenly, that car in front of you starts to move a little bit. A little perk of hope gets you feeling better. Then the car stops and you wait again. Maybe another ten minutes or so goes by, and the car starts to move a little bit again. That's one of those "little victories" we talked about earlier. But when we finally start on a slow roll, and then we can see the cars way in front of us moving at a decent pace, that's when we finally start to feel we are on the way to getting out of this jam. Deep down, we know we would not be sitting in the middle of all those cars for the rest of our lives, but we also had no idea how long we'd be there .

We are going to get out of life's predicaments one way or another, so why do we let them get us down? It's hard isn't it? Because we are right back in the middle of a new and different situation, a new jam, and we can't see a way out yet. Think about how much more fun life would be if we all could do better at this. Learning, taking the challenges as just that, a challenge, and not that "life" has it in for us and is out to get us. Keeping our chin up is not always the easiest thing to do, but when we keep it down, we just end up running into a wall.

I had a golf instructor tell me once that when you are in a fairway bunker (sand trap) and a long way from the green (your goal), make sure and keep your chin up. The reason is to be able to take a good full swing and let your shoulders rotate under your chin so you can make a solid strike and hit your target. Keeping your chin up not only helps you out when you are in a trap in golf, but it also works in life.

Now, what path are we going to take once we've made it out of a crisis or difficult situation? I have seen some of the most amazing people who have come out of very bad or difficult situations. Think about people who had been given up on, people who had been in some of life's worse situations, and went on to really make something of themselves. Have you ever stopped to think that it could be the people who have had to deal with more in life, who may actually be at an advantage over those who have not? We tend to feel sorry for people who have had hardships, but sometimes I think they have an extra springboard in life to launch them above all the rest. They are able to use all that strength and energy that they had to have to pull themselves up and use it to develop something very special in their lives. Sometimes it seems that those who just cruise along in life have nothing to spur them along or launch them into success.

But, sometimes it can be just as easy to take a path of discontent and frustration, allowing you to drop out of life. People will sometimes in these situations tend to reach for some type of vice or let themselves get caught up in a lifestyle that ends up destroying them. It's a choice.

Can't do it? Can't pick yourself up? Do you feel like you don't have the strength? Don't worry; you don't have to rely on our own strength. And it's a good thing we don't.

One of the hardest things for me when I was on the transplant list was each day knowing I was going to have to get on the treadmill. I had committed to my doctors that I would exercise at home. I was feeling so short of breath, and so weak, it didn't make sense to me to do that each day. It was hard enough for me to walk across the room, let alone be on a treadmill. It was probably the slowest walk anyone had ever seen, but I knew deep down I needed to do it. And with the oxygen cranked up, I was able to get by. I was supposed to walk thirty minutes each day. Some days I was real tempted to think that 20–25 minutes should be rounded up to 30 minutes. I had a CD player with a headset that I always used while I was on the treadmill. And there was a song by a group called Phillips, Craig, and Dean, and I think I pretty much wore out the CD and specifically this one particular song. There is a line in this song that kept me going for the thirty minutes on the treadmill, and I realized how important it is to stay as positive as possible during the tough times, and the key to getting through them came to me in this song. The line goes like this:

> And I will offer all I have
> So that His cross is not in vain
> His Cross will never ask for more than I can give
> For its not my strength but His

What a relief. I didn't have to rely on Randy's strength to get me through all this stuff that was going on in my life.

No matter what you're going through, you can make it. You can face the next day and push through whatever situation you are going through. Why? Because the strength that is inside of us is greater than any force that is outside of us.

CHAPTER 10

Setting And Achieving Your Goals

1 Corinthians 9:24

[24] Do you not know that in a race all the runners run, but only one gets the prize? Run in such a way as to get the prize.

I think everyone has goals in their lives. With some, it may be a very passive thought in the back of their mind. It might be a glimmer of hope or a dream to someday accomplish something. With others, goals are a very strategic, planned out, a written-down method in which they go about living their lives. In most all of my speaking engagements, I talk about goals. I feel it is an important aspect of our lives. They give us some specific direction and hold us accountable to ourselves.

I have been writing down my goals for the past several years. In fact, I really look forward to that part of the year when I look back at what I have accomplished, thank God for giving me another year, and then start to plan for the upcoming twelve months. I really work at carving out a method to get to where I want to go in my life. I keep my goals typed out on a small card and keep that card with me all the time. That way I can pull the goals out and read over them at anytime I need to. And with the system I use, I can look back at all the previous years too.

Do you have to write them down? Will it really make a difference if we do? I really believe so. One, it is a fun project each year. It really does give you an opportunity to reflect on where you have been, the big picture, and where you want to go. It also helps you to prioritize your life. Let's face it, we are all pulled in many different directions, and we need to be focused in order to be the most effective in the areas that are the most important to us. Sometimes it is hard to say "no" to others. Our time is very valuable to us, and we have people and organizations coming at us from many different directions. But, we have to realize that we often have to make our "yes" and "no" decisions based on what is best for us; otherwise we would never get to do what is important to us.

Now don't get me wrong, I am not going down a selfish road here, and I fully believe it is important to be helping out other people and organizations, but we need to make sure we are accomplishing what we need to as well. If there are a few specific groups of people or charities that you want to help, then put those on your goal lists, and stick to it so you don't get sidetracked. If someone else asks you for your time outside of the list you have committed to, you can simply tell them that your current list is full, and you really don't have any more additional commitments that you can allow this year in order to be fair to yourself and the other organizations.

Another reason why it is good to write down goals, besides being able to help you to prioritize, is that it will help you with your direction in life. Look at it like this. Let's say you take off in your car to go somewhere you have never been before. You have no idea of where it is or how to go about getting there. But, you still decide not to write down any directions or take a map. You may eventually find your way, but it might take you making a lot of wrong turns, or going out of your way and spending more time until you finally get to your destination. Not only is that time consuming, but pretty frustrating as well.

Now, let's say you take off for that same trip. You have it all mapped out, you have a plan, and specific notes on how to get there. You are serious about it. Your ideas are in place and you want to get to where you are going by the shortest route possible. It gets you there quickly and on target. You know you are going to have a better feeling of self-accomplishment because you were able to do what you wanted to do.

We all need direction in life. By having our goals in place they will act as these personal directions. They will help us not to get side tracked, and to obtain a better level of personal development, not only of ourselves, but our life in general.

Now, here is a very important key for when we write down our goals. Many people instantly think goals are all career or income based. That's not good. We all need a balance in our life, and this is a perfect way to help with that. Your list of ten or twelve annual goals will need to have balance. I break them down in these areas: spiritual, family, career, physical, and financial. There can be other variations of course, but this gives you a good idea on how to spread them out to cover several important areas.

Having spiritual goals can include things such as setting personal study time, reading the Bible, reading through the Bible in a year, having time for personal prayer. It may also be setting goals which will allow you time to spend helping others; volunteering at your church, helping out certain groups in your community, visiting people who are in need or in the hospital. Having goals based around "family" might include how you allocate time to spend with your wife, children, and parents. Making sure you don't miss out on the important things in life. Your career goals may be obvious. You might set a certain income level, you might be going after a promotion, you might want to have a priority that you help those around you to grow and have the chance for promotion. Your physical goals could mean ways you want to take care of yourself: achieving a certain weight, exercising, going on a diet, running a mile in a certain amount of time, shooting a certain score in a round of golf.

Now, there are also some real specific ways that we need to write these goals down. Don't ever use the words "I want to". For example, "I want to loose 15 pounds by the end of the year", "I want to get a promotion". We read that and it gives us the immediate impression of "maybe it will happen". It comes across as a wish, not a determined goal.

Instead, we need to write these goals down as a statement of authority, so when we read it, the goal will motivate us into action, not allow us to be passive. "I will loose 15 pounds by the end of the year" and if you then want to really be specific, under the goal list your detailed activities that you will do on a daily or weekly basis that will get you there. Hold yourself accountable; take charge of your life. Don't let others do it for you. If you are in charge of you life, it won't let others have the chance to do it for you.

Writing it down, sticking to it, and forcing yourself to do it, how can you not succeed? You might say, it's the sticking to it part that is so hard. Then get yourself an accountability partner. Even if they can't work out with you all the time or be there with you while you are eating each meal, you can still call them at the end of each week and report in to them how you did. You will have to own up to your results each week, but believe me, it will make a difference.

Lastly, if you really want to get the most out of goal setting, set up a prize or incentive for yourself when you accomplish your goals. Think about how a lot of companies have these great achievement club trips for their top performers. The people who finish at the top each year get awarded some type of special trip and usually a nice gift to go along with it. In my opinion, we should all be setting something like this for ourselves too. Make it fun, make your goals something that you want to hit and then reward yourself after you cross those finish lines. Get yourself a new outfit, a set of golf clubs, new running shoes, a weekend getaway, something to complement your achievement.

Think how enjoyable this process can become for you each year as you review your accomplishments, set new goals, and incentives, and then pay yourself off again.

CHAPTER 11

Why Me?

Nahum 1:7

[7] The LORD is good. When trouble comes, he is a strong refuge. And he knows everyone who trusts in him.

W e have all heard of the "why me" factor. I am sure we have all felt that way inside at one time or another, and probably said it out loud a few times too.

So, "why me?"

Why was Randy Sims born with this chronic disease, cystic fibrosis? Why did he have to grow up with some different challenges that other kids did not have to deal with? Why were his parents told at a young age that he might just have a couple more years to live? Why has he had to take all these medications every day? Why has he had to hear people say things to him like "you must feel like you are always walking on egg shells" or "why didn't you just give up a long time ago?"

I guess all these "whys" can be answered like this maybe:

Why not

I don't know

It doesn't matter

Why was I fortunate enough not to be in a worse situation?

I was fortunate to have this happen and have been able to learn so much from it all.

All of these are somewhat true, but there is a really simple explanation to why anything that is difficult in our life happens. You have heard me reference the Bible a few times already, so you know where my faith and belief lies. You can really learn a lot through faith and what is taught in the Bible. Does what we learn come instantly or easily?

Not necessarily. I believe the principles of the Bible are very straightforward; there are no gray areas. But, we do need to grow and mature as we take these beliefs to heart and begin to make them a center point of our life. I guess that is why it is such an exciting lifestyle and way of living. You are always learning and getting a deeper understanding of what is important. We keep striving to become better.

If we go back to the very beginning of time, I think everyone knows what happened with Adam and Eve. All was perfect, until that perfect bond was broken when they decided to go against God's will. Sin always has repercussions. So, do we blame Adam and Eve for messing up this perfect situation and state of paradise? I doubt it, since there has never been one of us who is sinless.

We all live in a world of sin and therefore suffer the consequences of it. Many times things don't seem fair. Many times these things cause us pain and sorrow. But trials will allow us to be refined. I learned a long time ago, when I asked for and received forgiveness, and made a conscious decision to turn my life over to Christ and do my best to live like Him, that no matter what happened to me here on earth, I would have my rewards in heaven for eternity.

But, how can we get through the "why me" syndrome here on Earth, day in and day out?

There are some things we have to do when we start feeling like this. And start doing them right away. Because, the more we let ourselves slip into this frame of mind, the deeper we get and the harder it is to get out.

I can tell you what I have seen work:

Prayer, consistent and specific.

Swallowing our pride and talking to someone about what it is that is getting us down. Seems easy but we just don't do it. And, I think 9 out of 10 times we do this, we are going to end up making the person we reach out to for help feel better about themselves too. Why? Because there is a good chance that they have felt or are feeling the same way, or going through something similar. So, now they also realize they are not alone. We have all had times in our life when we have felt alone. We could have been in a crowded room, or in a ball stadium full of people, and still felt this way. Just because we have a lot of people around us does not mean we are immune to feeling lonely. Probably one of the most common things that happens to us to make us feel this way is when we are dealing with something in our life, and we choose to keep it inside. We have a situation that we feel like we have to deal with all alone and choose not to let others into this area of our life. Or, maybe it is that we are dealing with something and we feel others just don't understand what we are going through. Or, we feel like we are the only ones who have ever had to deal with something like this. It could become a feeling that we are lost, and we just need some direction to get us back on course.

When I was growing up on the farm, my first day of riding the bus to school was a crazy adventure. I was a little apprehensive getting on the bus for the first time. The whole concept of riding with a bunch of strangers, and a guy that I didn't know who was supposed to get me to school, all the way from my home out in the country, that feeling was a little uncertain to me. But, the ride was pretty uneventful, and I made it just fine. But, then when I got on the bus to head home, I had a different bus driver for the return trip. I remember sitting in the back, and all the other kids had been dropped off. I was very anxious to get home. And, then I realized that the bus driver was lost. I was only in the first grade, and when you live in the country, it's not like you are a real expert on directions to your house. He wanted to know my address, I told him, "route #1". I guess that was not specific enough. So, I tried, "rural route # 1", and I don't think that helped much.

And, my final best effort for directions was to make a turn down the long gravel road and my house should be there. Of course there were no cell phones back then. And this poor bus driver just kept driving around until we figured it out together. Now, I have to say, that was a lonely feeling and it was easy to explain why I felt that way. But, as soon as I saw my house (two hours late), it went away. Just like in life, as soon as we see some sign of hope, the anxiety and feeling of being alone will start to drift away too.

But, sometimes we get this feeling that we can't really understand. It is a burning lonely feeling that just appears out of nowhere. I think it is one of those times that we are holding on to something that we need to get off our chest. We all need to have someone to talk to. And, if we are dealing with a certain challenge in life, it is a big help to find someone who has dealt with the same thing that we are going through. When I was on the waiting list to receive a transplant, it helped me a great deal to talk to someone who had been through the same thing. And after my surgery, it was also a big help to talk to those who had been on that side of it as well. You start wondering if a certain way you are feeling is normal, or a certain side effect is to be expected.

In dealing with CF, I was pretty private. I had a few close friends that I told, and would talk to them about it some, but overall, I pretty much wanted to go along in life and appear just like anyone else. Maybe that was not the best way to handle it? The bad thing there may have been parents in my town who had a child just diagnosed with CF that I might have been able to lend some advise to. Or talk to someone who was just diagnosed. It is the whole ideas behind support groups. I've decided not to keep what I've dealt with to myself anymore, with hopes that others can benefit.

Another way that helps to get through the "why me" feeling is to find some new and positive interests in life.

Focus on the positive that is around us (again, remember, the little victories each day) and not let the negative consume us. Surround yourself with positive activities and people whom you can count on to encourage you.

Get into life! Get involved. You have to take first steps and be willing to get into life. Just like you know you can't get new friends if you are not friendly to those around you.

Maybe you are in a position that you need to change something in your life, clean up in some area? Do you need to grow in a certain area?

Also, realize that what you are going through is not some type of punishment. It could be a wake-up call though.

Take this story for example. I was in a large department store shopping one day. I was looking for some new workout shoes. I noticed a large muscular guy shopping in the same row as I. Soon, from a few rows away I heard his wife call out to him "is our son with you?" He answered back quickly with a sharp concern in his voice, "no, I thought he was with you!" She quickly stated she thought the boy was with him. They immediately got together and started calling out the little boy's name. The father took off through the store franticly. A few moments later the dad was back with his little boy's hand tightly gripped in his. The son was crying. As the father entered back into the shoe department where I was, I heard him say to his child, "if you wander away from me again, if you think the punishment you just received was bad, it will be nothing compared to what you will get".

Interestingly enough, I noticed the tone of the father's voice was not anger; it was concern, and fear. He thought he had lost his son. The discipline he gave him was out of love, not anger. As hard as it was to discipline him, it would have been harder if he had done nothing and let his son wander off again and what if this time something tragic did happen to him and he never came back?

We can see a great parallel here, with the love of this father, and the love of our Heavenly Father. He does not want to lose us even more so than this father did not want to lose his child. And our loss would be much more tragic.

I like the old saying; rain softens the earth that we walk on, and it is that same rain that causes the plants to grow…we can also have rain in our life that may be intended to soften us up in some area so we can grow. Don't turn your back on the idea that what you are going through can actually help you make a positive change in your life and accomplish something new, something better than you already have. That it can cause your relationship to be stronger with your Heavenly Father as well.

There is a lot of truth to the old saying, "turn lemons into lemonade".

Speaking of "why me", one day when I was in the hospital for my annual check up, I was struggling with this and just decided to put myself in a bad mood. Have you ever done that? You know, there is not anything particularly wrong with your day, you just decide to analyze your situation and feel maybe you just deserve to let yourself be in a rotten mood. Teresa, my wife, was there with me. And she let me go on for about an hour like this. I am not sure why I was mad. I guess it was a nice spring day outside; I had the day off work to be at the hospital, and figured I deserved to be outside enjoying the day or some kind of logic like that. I guess I chose not to focus on the fact that I felt good, I was in much better shape than I could have ever imagined before my transplant, my wife had taken the day off too so we could be together. And my mom and dad had even decided to join us so they could catch up with some of the people that they had met at the hospital when I was going through the transplant. So, here I was, getting to have a day with my family, and really celebrating another year of good post-transplant health. But,

I was ruining it because I forced myself to be in an attitude that I didn't want to be there. Well, like I said, my wife let me act like this for about an hour. Then while we were sitting in one of the waiting rooms, she took hold of my ear and whispered some very good advice to me. She wanted to know what the matter was; of course, I had the normal male response, "nothing". And I think she pretty much knew what I was up to, and I eventually told her. What she said to me was that kind of advice that you hate to hear when you are "in the moment", but when you look back, it really made a lot of sense. She reminded me that I was not doing myself any good acting like this. And I sure was not focusing on all the good things that were going on in my life. Then, she also brought up another good point. There were a lot of people around me at the hospital, some who knew me (when you even get to know the parking attendants by name, you know you've spent a lot of time at the hospital). And when they saw me not wanting to visit with others and sitting around with my "arms crossed kind of attitude", I probably was not doing much for them either. They were probably thinking that I had just received some bad news from a test or something, or they were just trying to figure out what was wrong with me. At least I know I always feel bad for people when I see them in a waiting room not willing to speak or smile to anyone. So, each time I walk into the hospital for a check up, I think of that little pep talk. And, I know the attitude that I have can make a difference not only to me but others around me as well.

I am convinced there are two kinds of people, one that will wallow in their pity; the other is one that will wallow in their pity. Sound similar? In other words, we are all human and we all struggle with feeling sorry for ourselves from time to time. But the difference can come if we can learn to do it for a short time, and then pick ourselves up and get on with life. I guess there is a third type of person, who can pretty much shake anything off, and not let something bother them even for a short period of time. I'm not to that stage yet.

We just can't give up, we have to realize that the best is yet to come and right around the corner for us.

It's been said of those who have decided to end their own life, if they would have just waited a week, a month, or maybe even a few months, what they were going through that caused them to make that decision, would have come to pass. The situation would have gotten better. They would have been on their way to a new beginning. How sad. We've got to remember it is not our strength that we have to rely on to get us through these times. God's strength is much more than we can ever imagine. We just need to hold on through the storm, and the sun will shine brighter than ever once the clouds are cleared.

CHAPTER 12

Dealing With Those In Need

Proverbs 11:25

[25] A generous man will prosper; he who refreshes others will himself be refreshed

Sometimes it's hard to know what to say to someone who is going through a difficult time. Who are we kidding; it is always hard to know what to say. We all want to help, and we all have certain things we want to say, but never know how they are going to come across. We also genuinely want them to know we are there for them. Maybe someone is going through a family crisis, a job crisis, or a health crisis in his or her life.

Many times we will give the usual response, "let me know if there is anything I can do".

And that probably leaves the person wondering if they should ask for help or not. I think in these situations, the best thing we can do is to put ourselves in their shoes and think what we would want or need, and then make that suggestion. Suggest, "why don't I plan on coming by and I'll drive you to the doctor's office" or " If it's OK, we will bring a meal by your home Thursday evening". That lets them know you are going to help, and have already thought through what you want to do. Most people will never ask for something specific, but if we suggest one or two things that may open the door more and give them a comfort level to us to help.

Here is another important thing for us to remember. We cannot expect someone to be comfortable to talk about his or her situation if we come across not feeling comfortable. Do you get where I am going with this? Let me give you an example. Once I started getting older, I was pretty open when it came to talking about my health, especially if someone brought it up first. I want to be able to share information about my situation if there is anyway it might help someone else. I always told my doctors if there was another patient who needed someone to talk to, to please let me know. I had a lot of people who helped me along the way, and wanted to be able to do the same. I remember one occasion when Teresa and I were on vacation. We were out on a boat ride and were visiting with a family sitting next to us. In conversation on why we were on vacation, Teresa mentioned we were celebrating my "breath day", and explained that it was my anniversary from having a double lung transplant. Interestingly, the husband of this family kind of got a funny look on his face and changed the subject quickly and asked me "what kind of work are you in…"

I've done a lot of thinking about all the different things that people have said to me when they found out that I was on a waiting list for a transplant, or after my surgery. Changing the subject is pretty common actually. The funniest thing ever was when someone came in to see me at work and someone from my office said "Oh, Randy is competing in the US Transplant Games this week". He had known me for a while as a business acquaintance, but it had never come up about my transplant. So, they explained to him what all I had gone through. Well, when I came back from the 'games' and saw him the next time, he stopped in front of me and said "Wow, your staff explained to me about your lung transplant…" I just said, "Oh, OK". Then he went on to say, "so, you have two new lungs?" and I said "yes", and he just looked at my chest and said, "Well, they look great on you!"

I got a good laugh out of that.

Kidding around and jokes are much better than not saying anything at all. In fact, as I have thought back, it was the times that someone didn't say anything that made me the most uncomfortable.

So, I decided to put this is practice. The next time I was talking to someone, and asked how they were doing, and they dropped a "life bomb" on me, about a difficult situation they were going through, I decided instead of just saying the old "is there anything I can do...", or "I'm sorry to hear that" line, I'd engage in conversation with them. So, as I was asking them questions about the situation and talking to them about it, all of the sudden I could see some tension lift from their face. And I could see them becoming more relaxed in general. Understand this, if they see that it is OK for you to talk about it, and it is not scaring you or making you feel uncomfortable, they will hopefully feel the same. And, if they choose not to talk about it, they will let us know. But, at least we have bridged the gap, and hopefully broken down some barriers.

I get concerned when people feel they can't talk to anyone about a situation they are going through. It can lead them to a situation where they will feel they are backed into a corner.

Talking is always good, and getting others to talk is a great therapy. Sometimes we wonder what we can do when just being a good listener and getting a conversation going is the best medicine anyone could possibly get. Sending a card in the mail, leaving a voice mail, emailing a joke, dropping off a dinner, and sending a small gift are all important things we can do to let them know we truly care. Try not to do it just once, keep the encouragement going. Let them know they are not in this alone and you are in it with them for the long haul.

CHAPTER 13

Never Ever Give Up

Philippians 1:6

[6] being confident of this, that he who began a good work in you will carry it on to completion until the day of Christ Jesus.

Luke 18:1

[1] Then Jesus told his disciples a parable to show them that they should always pray and not give up....

Why do we seem to give up on so many things in life? I think it is because we can't see the good that is waiting for us just around the corner. But, we just can't let ourselves give up. This world is filled with great people who have made substantial contributions to society, and many of their lives were filled with extreme challenges and failure before reaching success. Just read the story of Abe Lincoln's life sometime.

But, in regards to failure, I for sure do not see a need for that word to be in our vocabulary. Does trying and not succeeding equal failure? Or, would never trying to begin with constitute the failure? Going through life without trying new adventures would be a real tragedy in my mind. And, if we succeeded in everything we tried, it would seem to take all the fun and excitement out of succeeding wouldn't it?

As children, we messed up on things all the time: learning to talk, walk, bathroom training. Good thing we didn't just give up and stop trying when we didn't get it right the first time, this world would be a mess. But, as we grow older, society seems to put these boundaries and pressures on us that we should never stumble or fall in our life's ventures.

Just look at all the tests and trials that have to go on to develop a new medication or medical procedure. I sure am glad that those who developed the transplant surgeries, and the medications needed to go along with it, did not give up, or I would not be here today.

Is it possible that the best things in life are actually the ones that are the most difficult to attain? Sometimes we simply do not have the choice to give up and we find ourselves in a situation in which we must push on. Those are great learning lessons for the rest of the areas in life.

Look at it like this. Take someone who has just been downsized by his or her company. Now, all of a sudden, their new job is finding a job. And, they find themselves in a position where they just can't throw in the towel. Sure, some days are going to be frustrating, some interviews will not go as well as they hope, and just when they feel they are about to get an offer, they find out the job went to someone else. But, they cannot give up. They have a family counting on them, and they know they have obligations to make this happen and to find a new career that they will enjoy.

Now, compare that situation to someone who is in a comfortable career. Maybe it's sales? And he or she find themselves in a slump. The deals are just not closing like they wish. The commissions are not coming in as they hoped. Really, this person is feeling the same frustrations as the person who is out looking for a job. But, the question is, will they just pull back and stay in this rut, or will they be able to find the same drive that the person who knows they have to push on and succeed or make the decision that it is time to move on and to land a new job? You have to be able to reach way down inside and overcome the feeling of frustration by pushing yourself past the "feeling of failure syndrome". If you keep telling yourself you are failing, you probably will, because you will give up. If you tell yourself that you just had a few bad breaks, and you know your luck will turn around, it probably will. You have to give yourself the best chance possible, and the only way you can do that is by having the right attitude.

Now remember once again, there is that difference between giving up and giving in! If you are in a career and you have exhausted all your drive, energy, and talents and it is just not getting you to where you want to go, there is nothing wrong with a change and giving in to trying something new. You didn't give up; you are just giving in to the idea that it is time for a change. There is a big difference.

Now there is one case where we will and must not ever give in or give up, and that is with "life". It can be so easy when we are in a slump in our life to let it keep getting us lower and lower. We simply can't let that happen at any cost.

We all go through dark times in our life. Life is going to be like a roller coaster. It will go back up and we will hear that "click, click" sound again. Great things are just around the corner for us. We just have to reach for that God-given strength to get us through.

You will make it. You are either going to make it in the current situation you are in, or you will figure out a way to change it around so it works out for you. Either way, you will make it!

CHAPTER 14

Celebrating

Romans 12:15

[15] Rejoice with them that do rejoice....

I've had many great things happen in my life since I went through my transplant. As I've often said, it's been much more exciting than the 32 years of my pre-transplant life. Meeting my wife Teresa just a year and a half after my surgery tops the list. We were married in Hawaii, a dream vacation that we both had. Now we enjoy traveling and vacationing, sporting events, and playing golf together, all things that I was unable to do for quite some time before my transplant. Getting involved with many different organizations and being appointed to the board of directors and executive board of directors for various organizations has been a great honor. I have competed nationally in the US Transplant Games four times, been published in several books and articles, and interviewed on different TV programs. Having the opportunity to travel throughout the country and speak to various organizations has also been a great thrill. None of these things would have happened if I had decided to throw in the towel and give up along the way. And never would I begin to take credit for being able to do any of these things on my own.

The US Transplant Games are a great venue to give thanks to the donor families and to also celebrate with many other recipients the "gift of life", as well as to compete in sporting events on a national level. The games are held in various locations throughout the Unites Sates and take place every two years.

Year 2000 was the first games that I attended, held in June; this was just a little over a year out from my transplant. It was a tremendous experience. My first flavor of what was in store was the opening ceremonies. They were held at the baseball stadium at Disney's Wide World of Sports. There were hundreds of athletes, transplant recipients, from all over the US marching in to take their seats for the opening ceremonies. Each state has a group of athletes just as the Olympics enter in the opening ceremonies with countries grouped together. The opening ceremonies are full of emotion, looking around at all of your peers who also share in the heightened awareness and appreciation of how precious life is, and how we all want to live it to our fullest. Then, once we were seated, all of the donor family representatives came in; there was a 20-minute standing ovation. What a moving tribute. The athletes, all organ recipients, standing and applauding those who have made decisions to give the gift of life and allow us to be there. This was a very emotional and beautiful scene. It's hard to describe the feeling. The organ recipients all sitting in one area, and many of their family and friends seated in the sections above them, then those who made it all possible for us the be there enter the stadium, and as the cameras focus in on them and they appear on the jumbo screens, you can literally feel the compassion and gratitude as it fills the arena.

The opening ceremonies included several speakers, music, fire-works, and a release of white doves to fly over the stadium, and of course, the lighting of the torch.

Then, the next three days were filled with the events. The first year I competed in racquetball and 3 on 3 basketball. Year 2002, I competed again in 3 on 3 basketball, and also golf and table tennis. There are about 20 events in all to choose from. Once the events were finished at the end of the week, the closing ceremonies took place. Again, another great show. I wasn't sure how my second set of games, year 2002, would compare to the first year I attended. I thought maybe the newness would kind of wear off and it would not be as special. But I was wrong. I got just as much, if not more excitement and thrill from the 2002 games and ceremonies as I did in 2000. This year was even more special because Teresa, my wife of just 6 months was there, also her family, and my brother and his wife came also. My parents were also there again. It's great for them to be able to see me compete in sports again, especially when there has been a lot of times that they have seen me not able to do much more than just sit in a chair connected to oxygen (pre-transplant days).

I guess to sum this up, it is a week filled with meeting strong, courageous people from around the country and celebrating the miracles that we have all been a part of. Drawing from each other's strength and understanding how better to deal with life's challenges. The days and nights are filled with sporting events, parties, seminars, ceremonies, food, and fun. There is always something to do for everyone, and always the chance to learn from each other. A lot of talk about what kinds of medications we each take, and what challenges or experiences we have gone through or are going through.

To me it's also a time to reflect on the love I have for my family and to remember how important my faith in God is. And of course, pay special tribute to all donors and their families.

I'll never forget how I first found out such a great thing even existed. I was sitting in the waiting room at the hospital, getting ready to have some routine post-transplant blood work done. And the person sitting next to me was also a recipient. She started telling me about this national competition that took place every two years. She went on to describe all these different events that were involved, and that there was this amazing opening and closing ceremony that thousands of people attended. It was almost too good to believe. And, what a motivation it was for me to get myself in the best physical shape possible.

One of the best things for me, as I continue to be involved each year, is now enjoying the absolute amazement from the recipients and their families as they attend for their first time. It is hard to describe all the emotions that go on that week as we pay tribute to all the donor families and the living donors. There have even been special occasions that have allowed seeing recipients meet their donor families for the first time, and that is truly amazing. It instills the positive affirmations of how well transplantation works and the amazing stories that have come from lives that have been saved through this wonderful process.

It's also a week when we can really focus on this miracle that happened in our lives. It is the vacation of all vacations, because you are able to concentrate not on all the day to day busyness that we all encounter, but take time to focus on: your family, your donor family, and the gift that we have all been given.

It's all about watching each other compete, and competing to win, but most of all competing just to compete. Some of the most amazing moments have been watching someone push him or herself just to finish a race. I also have really enjoyed the times that I have competed in golf. Golfing is always a great time to get to meet people, in this environment it is even better.

I remember the first games in the racquetball competition. I was 34 years old, and other than the training I had been doing over the last 6 months for the games, I had not played, nor was I really able to play racquetball since I was in college. But, I had joined a racquetball league at the YMCA, and had been playing competitively for a few months and had gotten to where I could beat some of the guys on the league, and they were pretty good. I thought for sure I would have a gold medal. I will never forget, I was walking in the court in Orlando with my dad, and told him that I'd be able to look at a few of the guys, size up my competition, and tell how I thought I'd be able to do and if I'd be walking out with the "Gold". As soon as we got through the front door, I saw two men in my age group warming up with each other; I was amazed at the level of play. My dad said, "what do you think", I said, " I think you can just leave the car running". I did win my first round; the person I was supposed to play didn't show up. The second round I played the guy who had won the gold medal the last few times. Wow, I swallowed my pride. But, I remember when I walked out of there; it gave me a good feeling. First of all, he was a great guy, who had overcome some amazing challenges. Second, it made me proud to know that he could have gone back and beaten any of the guys who were in my YMCA league. It was neat to see the level of competition that strong, and transplant recipients who were in that good of shape. And it just went to show, you don't have to win to have fun. Plus, different events have all levels of competition. Again, it's really about just getting out there and giving it a try that is the most important. In 2004 I medalled my first time, and in the 2006 games I took home both a gold and bronze.

As transplant recipients, we are very fortunate to have such an event, and the fact that it is on a national level makes it even more special. It keeps growing and growing in number of participants and spectators as well. And I am sure it will continue to grow. It motivates everyone to stay in shape; let's you enjoy those special times with your family, and allows you to meet some great people every time you attend. My wife and I, her family, and my family have all made it a tradition.

CHAPTER 15

A Special Tribute

Matthew 25:40

[40] The King will reply, 'I tell you the truth, whatever you did for one of the least of these brothers of mine, you did for me.'

How can you ever start to thank someone who has saved your life? How can you begin to express those words? That is how I felt shortly after my transplant surgery as I sat down to write a letter to my donor family. It was an anonymous letter; I sent it through my hospital, since I am not allowed to know who the family is, unless they choose to contact me. Maybe they will someday. I completely appreciate whatever their decision is as far as writing back or not. It was the hardest letter I had ever written though. I wanted to express my sympathy and at the same time show my gratitude. I imagine there was some sort of sudden tragedy that occurred to the person from whom I received my lungs. That is usually the situation. So, I was sure that they were going through a very difficult time of loss. Even though I do not know who this family is, or the person who was the actual donor, I think about them all the time. I am so grateful for the decision they made. A life giving decision made out of love, and compassion for others; and a decision that was made during a time of their extreme sadness.

I remember when I was only 16 years old; I was working in a clothing store. My boss then was a member of the Lions Club, a group that specialized in helping those who had lost their sight. They would provide braille books and that type of thing for those who were in need. He approached me one day with a donor card, asking if I would be a donor of my eyes. I didn't even know what that meant. And, back then lung transplants had not even been done yet, so I was not aware of anything like this. He explained to me that when I passed away, my eyes would go to someone that needed them, in order to give them their sight back. As he put it, I would not need them anyway once I was gone. It all made sense to me, and I signed the card. And, I am glad I had that opinion and feeling of giving back then, or I would have felt very guilty being in a situation of needing help in regards to an organ donor and transplant.

I want this family that gave my life back to me to know that I have not taken one day for granted since my new lease on life. And I truly receive this gift as just that, a gift of life. I want them to know that I feel a special obligation to do the very best to take care of myself, and not to take this lightly. And that their decision made an incredible impact on me, and I will never stop thinking of them.

It was very hard for me to come to grips with the whole idea of what would be happening to someone else in order for my life to continue. During my wait on the transplant list, I obviously had a lot of time on my hands, and spent a lot of time thinking about things like this. It was pretty overwhelming one day, and I remember talking to my brother on the phone about it. He brought up a good point, that if something happened to me or one of us in our family suddenly, we would for sure want to do the right thing, and hopefully have some good come of it and be able to help someone else. He was right. I knew each of us would feel that way. That helped me to put things in perspective.

The process of organ donation is so amazing. So many things have to fall into perfect place in order for a life to be saved. So many people involved at the hospital have to have a 100% focus on their job to make sure nothing falls through the cracks or is overlooked. I ran into my surgeon one day at Barnes-Jewish hospital, St. Louis. I told him how impressed I was with the entire process: the lab, the rehab center, the bronchoscope lab, the nurses and doctors on the post-op floor, the pilots who transported my lungs...

He said it was a matter of each person having the feeling that his or her job was the most important in the process, and knowing that if every step was not perfect, that the outcome would not be perfect. What a great philosophy.

The doctors and coordinators that have taken care of me both before and after my transplant have been fantastic. I have been so fortunate to have such great professionals so near to where I live.

But, again, as great as this entire process is, none of it would have been possible without the caring decision of the donor's family. I guess it was very late on April 8th, 1999, or very early in the morning on April 9th 1999, I was feeling at my worst, not sure if I was going to make it through another day or not, when a loving group of people chose to make a very unselfish decision. On April 8th, 1999, I never thought I'd be writing about all this, and what all has happened to me.

So now, if I can accomplish just one thing, it is to make you see there is hope.

Printed in the United States
62298LVS00001B/205-300

9 781595 940841